Angels
AMONG US

Angels
AMONG US

What the Bible Reveals about
Angelic Encounters

PERRY STONE

New York Nashville

FaithWords
Hachette Book Group
1290 Avenue of the Americas, New York, NY 10104
faithwords.com
twitter.com/faithwords

An expanded version of this text was originally published as *This Season of Angels* in hardcover and ebook in October 2018 by FaithWords

First Edition: September 2019

FaithWords is a division of Hachette Book Group, Inc. The FaithWords name and logo are trademarks of Hachette Book Group, Inc.

Unless otherwise noted, Scripture quotations are taken from the King James Version of the Holy Bible.

Scripture quotations marked (NKJV) are taken from *The New King James Version*®. Copyright © 1982 by Thomas Nelson. Used by permission. All rights reserved.

Scripture quotations marked (AMP) are taken from *The Amplified Bible*. Copyright © 1954, 1958, 1962, 1965, 1987 by The Lockman Foundation. Used by permission of Zondervan. The "Amplified" trademark is registered in the United States Patent and Trademark Office by The Lockman Foundation. Use of this trademark requires permission of The Lockman Foundation.

The publisher is not responsible for websites (or their content) that are not owned by the publisher.

The Hachette Speakers Bureau provides a wide range of authors for speaking events. To find out more, go to www.hachettespeakersbureau.com or call (866) 376-6591.

Library of Congress Cataloging-in-Publication Data has been applied for.

ISBNs: 978-1-5460-3526-8

Printed in the United States of America

LSC-C

10 9 8 7 6 5 4 3 2 1

CONTENTS

INTRODUCTION

This book details specific and unique aspects of angelic visitations, assignments, and ministry purposes, which most pastors seldom cover. I will reveal how we can and *should* believe God is sending angels to assist us throughout our life.

Before we begin, I wish to share the following practical insight based on the Bible:

1. Angels are real and are assigned for ministry. We often do not ask God for their assistance, but we should when we sense a particular need.
2. If Satan took one-third of the angels under his control during his rebellion, there are two-thirds that remained loyal to God. This fact indicates that for every evil agent in the kingdom of darkness, there are two angels that are *for* us. Thus, there are always more for us than against us (2 Kings).
3. The ministry of angels increases during prophetic seasons. It is clear that the powers of darkness will increase their intensity of war against the saints, as Satan knows he is running out of time (Rev. 12). We are told that where sin abounds, grace does

more abound (Rom. 5:20), and when the enemy comes in like a flood, the Spirit of the Lord will lift up a standard against him (Isa. 59:19). As the battle increases against dark forces, God will send his angels to engage in warfare.

In the following chapters, we will explore accounts of angels impacting the lives of people both in Scripture and in modern personal accounts. We will examine how angels communicate to us, in what ways they act in our lives, and how we can seek their blessings through prayer to the Lord. I will also answer unusual and controversial questions often asked about angels throughout the book.

My hope is that this book will help you to recognize how God uses angels as one of many ways to be constantly present in your life.

CHAPTER ONE

ANGELS OF HEAVENLY REVELATIONS

During the Old Testament dispensation, angels were needed in giving instruction and direction to God's people. The word "angel" (singular) is mentioned 201 times in 192 verses in the Bible, with 104 of those references found in the Old Testament. Angels traveled from the upper celestial realm with time-sensitive and life-changing information, giving direction and, at times, warnings, to patriarchs, prophets, and holy priests. It must be remembered that there was no law or written word from God from the time of Adam until Moses received the Torah (five books) on Mount Sinai—a stretch of 2,500 years. When a "word from God" was required, the message came through a spiritual dream or vision, a spoken word of inspiration, or through an angelic visitation.

The gospel is a curiosity to the spiritual realm as noted in the verse "angels desire to look into" (1 Pet. 1:12). When God descended to give Moses the law and the Commandments at Mount Sinai, David wrote, "The chariots of God are twenty thousand, even thousands of angels;

the Lord is among them, as Sinai, in the holy place" (Ps. 68:17). Angels surrounded Mount Sinai as God's Word was burned into the stone tablets.

The Angels Michael and Gabriel

In both the Old and the New Testaments, there is one noted angel, who during a 600-year time frame made personal visits to the Hebrew prophet Daniel in Babylon, to a Jewish priest at Jerusalem's Temple, and to a young virgin named Mary living in Nazareth. This angel is Gabriel, whose name means "Man of God." He is one of two angels mentioned by name in Scripture; the other being Michael the archangel (Dan. 12:1; Jude 9). Clearly, Michael is the highest-ranking angel in authority who also commands an army of angels (Rev. 12:7).

At Moses' death, Satan strategized to seize possession of his corpse. Not only did God send Michael to resist and rebuke Satan, but after Satan departed, God Himself scooped up the remains of Moses, placing Israel's greatest prophet in a private burial plot that remains a secret to this day (Deut. 34:6; Jude 9).

In a more dramatic face-to-face conflict, the prophet Daniel sought God for the interpretation of a strange vision he had received. However, the heavens were like cold brass. Daniel and his companions normally were a "one-day breakthrough" group—whether at the fiery furnace or the lions' den, when they ended up in dangerous places with death breathing down their necks, there an instantaneous deliverance always occurred. In the Daniel 10 narrative, three weeks of prayer and fasting had not penetrated the barrier that blocked the understanding that Daniel was seeking.

The issue was not that God was too busy to hear Daniel's prayer, or that God was testing him—He would just send the answer when He was good and ready. The problem was not found in the third heavenly realm, where God and angels join for heavenly counsels, nor was there some iniquity in Daniel's heart that could hinder his prayer (Ps. 66:18), as Daniel was a godly man. The standstill was headquartered in the second heaven, above Babylon, where two strong spirits—a demonic prince of Persia and God's special messenger (believed to be Gabriel)—were in a face-off where the powerful evil prince spirit attempted to restrain righteousness. His demonic interference seemed temporarily stronger, as it restrained God's messenger in the upper heaven from breaking through the earth's atmosphere. God observed this struggle of dueling angels and released His "secret weapon," who was on standby, waiting to fly like a rocket to the scene of struggle: Michael the archangel.

Michael entered the cosmic wrestling match and, using his superior authority, seized control of the demonic prince of Persia, immediately releasing Gabriel, God's messenger of revelation, to complete the assignment to which he was appointed.

As God's angelic messenger suddenly entered Daniel's prayer room, the prophet fell to the ground and the angel responded, "I have come for your words." These words were Daniel's prayer request to receive complete and perfect understanding of a mysterious vision (Dan. 10:1–2).

God's original plan was to release this information to Daniel on the first day of his prayer. The angel told Daniel:

> "Do not fear, Daniel, for from the first day that you set your heart to understand, and to humble yourself before your God, your words were heard; and I have come because of your words. But the prince of the kingdom of Persia withstood me twenty-one days; and behold, Michael, one of the chief princes, came to help me, for I had been left alone there with the kings of Persia. Now I have come to make you understand what will happen to your people in the latter days, for the vision refers to many days yet to come." (Daniel 10:12–14 NKJV)

There are two occasions when the angel Gabriel is mentioned by name as bringing prophetic understanding concerning the future to Daniel. The first is in Daniel 8, in which Gabriel reveals the animal symbolism seen in Daniel's vision and explains how each animal represents a future empire. A voice coming from the banks of the Ulai River tells Gabriel to "make this man to understand the vision" (Dan. 8:16).

In Gabriel's second appearance, he was seen by Daniel after the Medes and Persians overtook Babylon in a secret invasion. Daniel was reading the scroll of Jeremiah, which predicted that the Jews would return from Babylon after seventy years (Jer. 25:11, 29:10). Daniel was boldly repenting for Israel's sins and questioned if God would keep the promise of seventy years' captivity and transition the Jews from Babylon back to Jerusalem. To his amazement, Gabriel revealed a previously unknown prophetic cycle that would involve, not seventy years, but seventy weeks. This revelation of a new time required Gabriel to explain the detailed division of the seventy weeks. We read:

Now while I was speaking, praying, and confessing my sin and the sin of my people Israel, and presenting my supplication before the LORD my God for the holy mountain of my God, yes, while I was speaking in prayer, the man Gabriel, whom I had seen in the vision at the beginning, being caused to fly swiftly, reached me about the time of the evening offering. And he informed me and talked with me, and said, "O Daniel, I have now come forth to give you skill to understand. At the beginning of your supplications the command went out, and I have come to tell you for you are greatly beloved; therefore, consider the matter, and understand the vision." (Daniel 9:20–23 NKJV)

An interesting insight is in the sentence "At the beginning of your supplications the command went out, and I have come to tell you…" This phrase conceals a dynamic *prayer revelation*. The supplication, which alludes to Daniel's prayer request, ascended from Babylon to God's throne without any time delay or demonic resistance. God's response was immediate and the phrase "the command went out" refers to God's direct instruction to bring the answers Daniel was praying for. This indicates that God commands angels to bring certain messages and insights at specific times. Gabriel's urgency to inform the prophet is noted as he began to "fly swiftly," to Daniel's prayer location in Babylon.

In the English translation of the King James Bible, the word "fly" is found twenty-two times, and five different Hebrew words are used. The common word means "to fly like a bird." The word "fly" used in this Daniel reference is *ya'aph* and has a root that refers to being "wearisome, as by flight." This word indicated that as God's angels were moving toward Daniel, there was a conflict that would create a wearisome situation in the movement of the angel. Just as a human would become weary from nonstop battle day after day, the angel was in a literal wrestling match for three weeks in the heavenly realm.

The prophetic revelations that Gabriel released to

Daniel in chapter 11 concerning the future are so precise and detailed that only God Himself could have aligned future events that came to pass in history. Why is Gabriel selected as God's primary messenger to announce important revelations to specific individuals? The answer is found in an appearance of Gabriel from the New Testament.

Luke expounds on two narratives in which Gabriel is directly involved in explaining the conception of two sons: John the Baptist and Jesus. The first story unfolds at the Temple in Jerusalem, where the priest Zacharias is chosen to burn incense on the golden altar in the Holy Place, only to be interrupted by an unexpected visitor who is standing at the right side of the altar, which is traditionally the side reserved for God Himself. The angel says, "I am Gabriel that stands in the presence of God" (Luke 1:19). As Gabriel stands in God's presence, he is aware of God's plans, strategies, and prophetic purposes on earth. Gabriel knows the secrets of heaven, the mysteries of God, the strategies of angelic assignments determined in the heavenly counsels and reported those plans to men on earth throughout Biblical history. Gabriel knew that Zacharias and his wife had prayed for a son, and God had heard their prayer. Gabriel released the details: Zacharias would have a son named John (Luke 1:13), and the child would be filled with the Spirit from his mother's womb, and he would minister in the spirit of Elijah to prepare the way for the Messiah (Luke 1:15–17).

Gabriel's knowledge of this information was not "new" to him, as the Old Testament prophets had penned predictions of John's mission in Isaiah 40:3: "The voice of one crying in the wilderness to prepare the way of the Lord." Four hundred years before John's birth, Malachi wrote in Malachi 3:1 to reaffirm that God would send a messenger to prepare the way of the Lord. This was John the Baptist's assignment. When the time did arrive, Gabriel was sent to the future parents to give the additional details known only to heaven.

Six months later, Gabriel's most significant revelation was disclosed in the tiny town of Nazareth, a village community where some scholars believe perhaps thirty families lived. In a visit that would be recounted in every generation, till this day, Gabriel appeared to a teenage virgin named Mary. He indicated that she would supernaturally conceive the seed of God through the Holy Spirit's power. Her son, Jesus, would be called the Son of God and become the world's savior (Luke 1:31–33). The predictions spoken by Gabriel were fulfilled in detail through the ministry of John and Christ.

False Angels of Revelation

A firm warning should be noted here. Because the Jews in Paul's day knew how significant the ministry of angels was in bringing God's word to earth, Paul also gave believers cautionary advice when he wrote: "But even if we, or an angel from heaven, preach any other gospel to you than what we have preached to you, let him be accursed" (Gal. 1:8 NKJV).

Why would Paul warn of angels preaching another gospel? In context, his warning covered the danger of false prophets entering the church, introducing new revelations contrary to the pure Gospel of Christ. Some heretical doctrines in Paul's day included the teaching that Jesus was an angel and not a man, that Christ was not the Son of God, or that He was only a mortal who had not preexisted with God. Hebrews 2:2 says, "For the word spoken by the angels was steadfast…" True angels will always agree with the revealed, written Word of God.

During the past 1,500 years, two noted religions have made claims to be birthed through spiritual revelations given by angels to their founders. The main challenge to these theories is that both of these religions teach certain doctrines or concepts that are contrary to the sacred Word of God.

The first is Islam, whose founder, Muhammad, alleged that the angel Gabriel appeared to him, bringing him new spiritual revelations for those living in Arabia. At first, Muhammad appeared to be friendly toward Jews and Christians, until they rejected his claim as a prophet. The sayings of Muhammad are written in Islam's main book, the Quran. There are verses in the Quran that agree with the Scripture, such as Mary being a virgin and Jesus being conceived through divine means. Islam also accepts Jesus

as a prophet. However, the significant difference between
Biblical Christianity and Islam is that, according to the
angel's message in the Quran, Jesus is not the Son of God
as "Allah (God) cannot begat a son." Whatever possible
angelic manifestation Muhammad received, the doctrine
of Jesus not being the Son of God does not agree with the
message of Gabriel, who appeared to Mary and declared
that Jesus would be "called the Son of God" (Luke 1:35).
The answer most Muslims give to explain this contradic-
tion is that the Jews and the Christians changed the Bible
to make it read in agreement with their doctrine. There
are numerous theological and historical differences in
certain Islamic beliefs and the Scripture.

The second major religion, headquartered in the
United States, claims that its sacred book, the Book of
Mormon, was translated from gold plates hidden in the
Hill Cumorah by an angel named Moroni in New York
State. The angel allegedly led Joseph Smith to the concealed location, and Smith peered through two stones
to interpret the ancient language on the plates identified as "reformed Egyptian," now extinct. The message
was printed in the Book of Mormon and claims that
two groups of people migrated to America before the
time of Christ and eventually extinguished each other
in battle.

There are many good, moral Mormons who have a
love for God. However, the question remains: Was the
Book of Mormon inspired, or is it a man-made novel

that was marketed as a divine revelation? There are numerous verses in the Book of Mormon that contradict proven Biblical doctrines, all of which have been exposed by knowledgeable evangelical scholars. Finally, the angel of revelation who supposedly appeared to Joseph Smith was not an angel of the Lord with some new revelation—I believe this is an example of what Paul alluded to when he warned believers not to heed the words of any angel who would bring a new or another gospel.

The Purpose for Any Revelation

Any angel sent from God never contradicts the Holy Scriptures. However, Paul taught that Satan can "transform himself as an angel of light," thus converting his ministers into "ministers of righteousness." The context here is Paul warning the church of false apostles and deceitful workers infiltrating the church at Corinth (see 2 Cor. 11:13–15).

The purpose of "angelic revelation," especially in the New Testament, is often to bring either a warning of coming danger or some type of necessary instruction related to God's will. For any believer, the most important path in our journey is where God's perfect plan will lead us. In this dispensation, we are blessed to have the Holy Spirit working as our helper (Rom. 8:26), quickening our understanding toward God's Will. The Word of

God is His complete revelation to mankind, revealing future events and the plan of redemption through the Messiah, Jesus Christ. Angels were involved in the process and continue to be involved in ministering to the people of God.

HOW CAN WE DISCERN WHEN AN ANGEL IS IN A ROOM, OR WHEN WE ARE IN THE PRESENCE OF AN ANGEL?

There is a difference when the Holy Spirit is felt and when an angelic agent is in the room or the sanctuary. The presence of the Holy Spirit moves "out of your belly" (John 7:38), or within your inner spirit, flowing from inside to outside. When the woman from the Bible touched Christ in faith, the Lord said that someone touched Him because he felt "virtue" (literally power) leave his body. When you sense the Spirit of God, it will be inward first.

However, the presence of an angel of the Lord is always outward. You have the perception that you are being watched, that someone is in the room and you can't see them, but you know they are there. Angels can be detected through the gift of "discerning of spirits" (1 Cor. 12:7–10). Most charismatics believe this gift is to discern the presence of demons possessing a person. This is part of the operation of the gift, but notice it is "spirits," plural. This gift also enables the receiver to detect the presence of angelic beings.

In the Bible, when angels were seen, there was an overpowering presence of God and a holy reverence that often overwhelmed people, causing them to fall prostrate. During my lifetime I have experienced the presence of angels. Many people have asked what it was like and how I knew it was an angel.

First of all, the location in which the Divine Presence is sensed is important. The Holy Spirit lives within us and His activity moves inward to outward. When we pray in the Spirit, our (inward) spirit is praying (1 Cor. 14:14). As Christ taught, the river of life flows out of our "belly" or inward man (John 7:38). When an angel enters a room, the presence is around you and not just in you. The entire atmosphere shifts, and there is always a strong sense of the holiness of God.

In nearly every angelic visitation I've experienced, I began to cry and felt as though I should not move. Those who have known our ministry for years have on occasions been in a service where we know God had sent an angel into our presence. It is so evident that even those who are a bit more skeptical are seen trembling, weeping, or in awe. Some (such as my father) would describe it like invisible electricity in the air. I am sure this is because these spiritual agents have been in God's presence and they carry it with them.

The second "change" I have always sensed is a peace that settles over the room and myself. If your spirit is troubled, there will be the most marvelous sense of peace that will "charge" the room. When this peace manifests, there is not a care in life that is stronger than what you feel. It is as though everything melts away.

The third point would be there is also a unique strength that replaces any fatigue or weakness of the mind, spirit, or flesh when the angelic presence departs. On several occasions I was so physically exhausted from ministering, that I was uncertain if I could carry on. Suddenly I felt that outward presence and knew an angel of God was visiting. Once the presence lifted, a new strength settled over me. There was mental clarity, spiritual renewal, and physical strength. I can assure you that when you are in the presence of the Divine, you will know, as it will be pleasantly different from anything you have experienced before.

CHAPTER TWO

ANGELS IN DREAMS AND VISIONS

The twenty-seven New Testament books are filled with unique stories of angels bringing instructions and warnings through dreams or visions. Most people experience dreams during their sleep and a few have experienced visions. A vision differs from a dream. If a person dreams, they may not be aware they are actually sleeping or in a dream state, until they awaken. A vision, however, presents itself in a clear, full-color, and three-dimensional way and is so well defined, it is as though you're awake and your eyes are open. The details of a vision are precise, and your five senses are in full operation.

Visions of Angels

At the same time, dreams have changed the outcome of major events. When Mary conceived the seed of God's Word, Christ, Joseph was an honorable and righteous man who was preparing to give her a bill of divorcement, since he was not the father. It was the message of an angel in a dream that interrupted the plans of Joseph and instructed him to take Mary as his wife (Matt. 1:20). Joseph followed the instruction, as it is written, "Then Joseph being raised from his sleep did as the angel of the Lord had bidden him, and took unto him his wife" (Matt. 1:24). If Joseph had failed in this mission, Mary would have still birthed Christ but the circumstances surrounding his birth would have always been questioned, especially if she did not have a husband. There were laws in the Torah that Moses wrote that stated a child born through fornication or adultery could not enter the congregation of the Lord to the tenth generation (Deut. 23:2). Joseph should be admired and thanked for his willingness to listen to the angelic dream.

Joseph's second angelic dream was after the Christ child was born. Herod, the jealous ruler of Judea, was threatened by the infant Christ's destiny to be king. In an envious rage, Herod lost control and went on a killing rampage, ordering soldiers to slay all infants under two years of age in and around Bethlehem. This death decree placed Christ in the target of Herod's death squad, initiating God to set up an escape strategy for the holy family. In a dream, an angel of God told Joseph to take the young child and His mother to Egypt (Matt. 2:13–15).

It would be months later, when a third directional dream was revealed to Joseph, once again by an angel of the Lord, telling him to bring the family back to Israel, as Herod was now dead and his plot was no longer a threat (Matt. 2:19–21). This angelic command to return fulfilled a prophecy in Hosea 11:1: "Out of Egypt I have called my son."

In each of these three narratives involving Joseph, the Old Testament prophets pierced the veil of the future. Isaiah knew the Messiah would be born of a virgin (Isa. 7:14); Hosea said God's "son" would be called out of Egypt (Hosea 11:1), and when the family departed from Egypt with the intent of living in Judea, Joseph instead moved to Nazareth in Galilee, which fulfilled numerous prophecies, revealing that Galilee would produce a light for the Gentiles (Isa. 11:10; 49:6). Joseph's obedience to the angelic dreams is to be commended, as it placed Christ in the right place at the right time and protected Him from a premature death.

Angels Connect People

The ministry of angels was activated during the formation and growth of the early church. At the time of the early acts of the apostles (recorded in the book of Acts), the New Testament we have today was not written and compiled into one book. The New Testament canon would later be approved by the church counsels to be made into twenty-seven books. In Acts, angelic activity is consistent as angels are seen delivering the apostles, warning individuals in dreams, and connecting people for the kingdom of God.

In Acts 10, a Roman centurion was praying when an angel in "bright clothing" (Acts 10:39) appeared and gave him the good news that his prayers and charitable contributions had come before God as a memorial (Acts 10:4). This angel was in the process of connecting two men—a Gentile named Cornelius and a Jewish apostle, Simon Peter.

At this time in history, devout Jews had no dealings whatsoever with Gentiles. Thus, it required a supernatural event or divine encounter to connect these two opposing ethnic groups. Cornelius was instructed to send men to Joppa and inquire about a man named Simon Peter who resided in the house of Simon the Tanner near the Sea (Acts 10:30–32). Notice the details given by the angel: Peter's location in Joppa; the owner of the house where Peter was staying, a man named "Simon" who was "a tanner"; the home being situated near the (Mediterranean) Sea. Joppa was a large seaport city, and when these men journeyed to the region, they needed such details, including the man who was assigned to bring Cornelius a gospel message: "Simon whose surname is Peter" (Acts 10:5).

In order to prepare Peter to minister to these Gentiles, he experienced a strange vision, a sort of "illustrated message," in which God informed him that what He called clean, Peter should receive. Moments later a knock on

the door confirmed the meaning of the vision and Peter
began a journey into new territory that would alter the
course of spiritual history, and would introduce the Gentiles into the redemptive covenant (Acts 10:10–21).

Based upon Jewish cultural restrictions of fellowship-
ping with Gentiles, had an early prophet in the church
"prophesied" to Peter that God chose him to meet and
preach to this Gentile family, Peter would have likely
rejected the idea. The details from the angel were so
precise and confirmed by Peter's own spiritual vision,
that he understood the visit and his obedience fulfilled
the sovereign plan of God.

Angels Revealing the Will of God

It was a night vision that I experienced in 1988 that
set the course for our worldwide ministry that today is
reaching millions. Early one morning while in a deep
sleep, I suddenly found myself in a full-color, three-
dimensional vision. I was standing at the bottom of a
set of old concrete steps that led to the top of a small
hill, where I observed a tall metal television tower with
small round satellite dishes attached midway up the
structure. To the left side, I clearly saw a man, about six
feet four inches tall, dressed in a black suit, a white shirt,
and a dark tie. A strange feeling that I would describe
as a "holy awe" settled over me. The man lifted his left

hand to the metal tower, pointing his index finger to the dishes, then said to me, "If you will do these three things, then God will give you this." He proceeded to give me three direct instructions, including one that was personal and two that emphasized the importance of my total obedience to God in the ministry.

When the vision faded, I knew by inner revelation that the tower was somehow linked with television and the satellite dishes would carry my messages around the world. Yet I did not own any type of video or television equipment, much less cameras or a studio.

Two years later, the growth of our outreach ministry required a much larger facility and land for future development. After weeks of searching, I came across eighteen empty acres, and while walking through the tall grass, I was stunned to come across the exact concrete steps leading up the knoll that I saw in the vision. On this property now sits the Voice of Evangelism headquarters and the studio for producing our weekly *Manna-fest* telecast. The place where the man stood in the vision is today the place where the gospel is being preached and heard around the world.

Both Dad and I believed that the person in the vision was an angel in the form of a man sent to earth to reveal what would occur in the future of the ministry, as the information was an unknown plan and a revelation directly from God.

Recognizing Angels

If an angel appears in a dream, don't necessarily expect to see a glowing creature in white with large feathers like wings flapping in your face. This is the common image of an angel, as often displayed on canvas oil paintings, in older Bible etchings, and in modern movies. Angels in their spirit bodies can have wings (Isa. 6:2–3), but in human appearance, they take the forms of men.

In a dream, an angel can appear in the form of a normal-looking man. It is important to note several things:

1. How does the "person" address you in the dream or vision—as "son" or "daughter" or by your name? Angels will use both "son" and "daughter" and the common name of the person.
2. What information is revealed? Is it a direct warning or a revelation of what will occur in the near future?
3. Is the revelation given in line with the Word of God? If not, it should not be feared, revered, or accepted, as angels always "harken to the voice of God's word" (Ps. 103:20).

Some theologians suggest that there is no need for any type of "revelation," since we have the Scriptures, which is basically true. However, I have noted there are many important decisions that must be made in life that can only be revealed through prayer and revelation. The Bible teaches that we should marry a believer, but only by "revelation" (understanding something unknown) can you know who is the right person. We are told that God will bless the works of our hands; however, the Bible never says where to live and work. This must be made known by the leading of the Holy Spirit through prayer. Being at the right place at the right time enables a person to meet others (or kingdom connections) that are assigned to open doors for your future. The Bible certainly reveals how to morally and spiritually live, how to treat others, and how to respond in negative situations. It does not tell you how many children you should have as this is made known as God directs the formation of your family.

Paul told the church at Corinth he would speak by "revelation, knowledge, prophesying, or by doctrine" (1 Cor. 14:6). Paul prayed the church would receive the "spirit of wisdom and revelation in the knowledge of him" (Eph. 1:17). In Acts 8, Phillip was preaching in Samaria when an angel of the Lord spoke to him to travel to Gaza (ninety-four miles away), where Phillip met an Ethiopian eunuch who was under Queen Candace's authority, who was converted to Christ and baptized in water (Acts 8:26–40). This conversion was significant as many of the Christians in Ethiopia trace their roots to this one man who tradition says assisted in the spread of Christianity in the region. In Acts 27, the vessel in which Paul was sailing hit a storm lasting fourteen days and the ship began falling apart. An angel of the Lord appeared at night giving a three-fold revelation:

1. The ship would be destroyed but none of the men onboard would die (Acts 27:22).
2. Paul would be cast upon an island for a brief time (27:26).
3. Paul would eventually end up in Rome to witness to Caesar (27:24).

All three predictions came to pass and Paul ended his ministry in Rome (Acts 28). With the Word of God and the influence of the Holy Spirit within each believer, we can receive spiritual downloads and know things to come by revelation of the Spirit. However, God can and does send angels in dreams and visions to at times send important messages, always pointing the visionary to Christ and God's will.

WHY DO SOME ANGELS APPEAR AT TIMES AS CHILDREN?

It is a bit difficult to explain angels that appear as children, as the Scripture is silent on this subject. While there is not any Scripture where angels appear as children, there are countless stories of children appearing to believers who were, in reality, angelic visitors.

The concept of children as angels is often connected with the Scriptures that Christ spoke of, where the angels of children behold the face of the Father in heaven (Matt. 18:10). In medieval times, it was common for artists to paint infants with wings, or "baby cherubim," as some believed that when an infant died, their spirit was transformed into a baby angel. When David's infant son (the child of Bathsheba) died seven days after his birth, David said he could not bring him back, but would instead go where the child was. He was not speaking of going to the grave, but was alluding to paradise, where the righteous souls go after death (2 Sam. 12:23). The spirit of the child had departed from his body and was with other righteous souls in paradise. He was not transformed into an angelic being, but will be raised at the resurrection of the dead and given an immortal body in the future, as will David and all righteous souls who died in covenant with God and Christ.

There are numerous mysteries connected to the realm of spirits, both evil and angelic. One moment, they can appear in spirit form, and other times as a "man." Other times, they manifest in a dream or a vision, with bright white remnants or in a flaming fire. These various forms give us a clue that angels can change their appearance. Because of this unique ability, there is the possibility they can appear in younger forms, such as a child, but only if there is a specific purpose for this kind of manifestation.

CHAPTER THREE

ANGELS WHO APPEAR TO US

We know that angels are spirits, and to the human eye, they are invisible; yet in their own realm, they can be seen by all other spirits on the same level. Satan is not invisible to God, the Holy Spirit, Christ, or other angelic beings, just as God is not invisible to all forms of demonic agents. Spirits can actually take on different forms in their realm. Spirits are in a completely different dimension than humans, and with their ability to travel at the speed of thought (more on this in chapter 7), they can create the appearance of light, brightness, and fire. One logical reason for invisibility is that the speed at which they travel is too fast for human eyes. We would have to have a veil lifted to be able to see the upper realms.

Angels in Human Form

Long before social media, cell phone pictures, and advanced recording technology, most stories outside of news agencies were repeated by word of mouth. After being passed from person to person, the original content becomes so embellished at times that the event is unrecognizable to the person who first reported it. Some of the early stories rumored in the late 1970s and early 1980s told of a male hitchhiker who was picked up by Christians. As they drove together, the unnamed man would announce, "Jesus is coming soon," and suddenly disappear from the car. I heard this story repeated through the years and the location where the man was hitchhiking continually changed. After numerous attempts to trace down the story's origin, I finally gave up.

While I am uncertain of the accuracy of this hitchhiker story, the fact remains that the Bible teaches that angels can at times take on the form of humans. One verse is Hebrews 13:2: "Do not forget to entertain strangers, for by so doing some have unwittingly entertained angels" (NKJV). The Old Testament records numerous examples of how "men" that spoke, ate, and performed specific duties were in reality angels sent on unique assignments.

During the first 2,500 years of human history, there were extraordinary angelic manifestations on earth, especially in the Promised Land, where angels appeared in the form of a man. One of the most noted instances was when God sealed the day of judgment against Sodom to destroy the wicked cities, yet was restrained by the fact that Abraham had close family members living in the cursed city. The law of God later confirmed that in the mouth of two or three witnesses let every word be established (Deut. 19:15; Matt. 18:16). The Lord and two men visited Abraham to warn him of God's decision to eradicate the evil that had emerged from the people in Sodom, corrupting surrounding cities.

After a generous meal, and a series of negotiations concerning the possible destruction of Sodom, the Lord instructed the two "men" accompanying him to journey to Sodom to confirm if ten righteous individuals remained among the wicked in the city (Gen. 18). These two men were actually angels taking on human form and were not recognized by the population in Sodom (Gen. 19). Only when these two strangers supernaturally blinded the men of Sodom at the door of Lot's house to prevent them from violently raping Lot, did they realize they were dealing with two beings from another world.

Another example is when Jacob was left alone and he "wrestled a man to the breaking of day" (Gen. 32:24). This "man" proved to be an angel of the Lord whom, at the conclusion of the wrestling match, put a blessing on Jacob, changing his name to Israel. Afterward we read: "And Jacob called the name of the place Peniel: for I have seen God face to face, and my life is preserved" (Gen. 32:30).

In all angelic appearances to people and in dreams and visions, the angel always appeared as a man. The only example of an angel looking like a woman is when Zechariah describes angels carrying a woman in a basket to the land of Shinar: "Then I raised my eyes and looked, and there were two women, coming with the wind in their wings; for they had wings like the wings of a stork, and they lifted up the basket between earth and heaven" (Zech. 5:9).

Twice Daniel saw Gabriel, normally invisible, and this mighty angelic prince stood before him "in the appearance of a man" (Dan. 8:15). In Daniel 9:21, Daniel records another encounter with the same messenger and writes, "While I was speaking in prayer, even the man Gabriel, whom I had seen in the vision at the beginning, being caused to fly swiftly, touched me..." (Dan. 9:21). In both visitations, Gabriel is called out by name, but is called "the man" by Daniel—not because the Bible is describing a human, but because Gabriel appeared in a human form.

Gabriel also appears twice in the New Testament. In the Temple's holy place, the priest Zacharias saw "an angel of the Lord standing on the right side of the altar of incense" (Luke 10:11). In this instance, Gabriel is not reported to look like a *man* but is identified as an *angel*. This is not to say Gabriel did not possess similar human features, but there was something noticeable that caused the priest to understand that this was a being from another dimension, sent from God. Also notice that because of Zacharias' unbelief, Gabriel had the authority to cause him to go mute during the entire nine months of his wife, Elizabeth's pregnancy (Luke 1:19–20).

The second appearance of Gabriel was in Nazareth to a teenage virgin named Mary. As Gabriel approached Mary, he called her "highly favored and blessed among women" (Luke 1:28). This greeting confounded Mary, and she was informed she would bring forth a son, a savior, named Jesus. Her only question was how she, a virgin, would give birth without a man? The angel told her He would be conceived through the power of the Holy Spirit. Mary did not reason, question, or doubt, but said, "Be it unto me according to your word" (Luke 1:38). I am certain she knew this messenger was not earthly, as Gabriel's message was part of the Messianic expectations that were predicted hundreds of years earlier by certain prophets.

Just as Christ sent forth his disciples two by two, angels can at times minister in groups of two, especially during significant prophetic seasons or when national destinies are altered. At Christ's tomb and the ascension, the angels were in groups of two. Two angels went to Sodom (Gen. 19); in Babylon, Michael the archangel and Gabriel were traveling from heaven to earth bringing messages or battling strong prince spirits that attempted to disrupt God's plan for Israel and the Jews (see Dan. 10).

During the season of the Old Testament Judges, when God was dealing with Israel and raising up men and women as deliverers to free the tribes of Israel from their internal and surrounding enemies, angels would be directed with specific encouragement and plans that, when followed, initiated supernatural deliverance from their enemies.

In the book of Judges, an angel appeared to rebuke Israel for their lack of total obedience (Judg. 2:1–4). An angel was involved in defeating the king of Canaan and made it known while praising Jael, a woman who took it upon herself to slay an enemy king (Judg. 5:23–24). Gideon was called into battle through the advice of an angel of the Lord who performed signs and wonders before Gideon to confirm he was going to defeat an invading Medianite army (Judg. 6:11–22). God released an angel of revelation to the mother of Samson, giving her instructions that her son would be a Nazarene and deliver Israel (Judg. 13). This angel also gave special signs to confirm the words he had spoken (Judg. 13:20). Once the message was given and heard by the future parents, we read, "But the angel of the Lord did not more appear to Manoah and to his wife. Then Manoah knew that he was an angel of the Lord" (Judg. 13:21). All these angels appeared as men and some were thought to be men, until they performed a miracle of an amazing feat and would suddenly disappear.

Angels Taking on Other Forms

Angels can take on other visible forms that are not human. In some instances, the difference is subtle. In many angelic visions, especially in Daniel, the angelic messenger takes on the appearance of a man (with head, arms, legs, and bodily features), but the angel's face flashes like lightning and his eyes appear as fire with feet similar to bright polished brass (Dan. 10:6). At Christ's resurrection, the angel who rolled the stone away from the tomb is described with a countenance as lightning, and clothing as white as snow (Matt. 28:3). The guards were afraid and fell to the ground as dead men (Matt. 28:4).

Other angelic spirits take on drastically different forms—forms so unusual their description is difficult to explain. Angels called cherubim have dual faces, that of a man and a lion with feet similar to the feet of calves (see Ezek. 1 and 10). The cherubim alluded to in Ezekiel's visions (see Ezek. 1 and 10) are described as a disk like a wheel full of eyes with a life force energy emanating from its center (Ezek. 1:20).

Isaiah in his vision saw God's throne room surrounded with angelic beings worshipping the Almighty. Identified as "seraphim," each had six wings, three on each side, with two covering their eyes, two their feet, and two used for flying (Isa. 6:2–3). Their ministry is to worship God, reminding all heavenly creatures that God is "Holy" (Isa. 6:3). In Revelation, John describes four "beasts," or living creatures, surrounding God's throne with the faces of an ox, a lion, an eagle, and a man (Rev. 4:7). The assignment of these unique heavenly creatures is the same as the seraphim, to worship and announce the holiness of the Lord (Rev. 4:8).

Though not an angel, when the Holy Spirit descended upon Christ, the Bible says He came "like a dove" (Matt. 3:16). Luke added more detail when he wrote, "And the Holy Spirit descended in the bodily shape like a dove" (Luke 3:22). All four gospel writers indicate this was the Holy Spirit and not just a manifestation (Matt. 3:16; Mark 1:10; Luke 3:22; John 1:32). We assume the Holy Spirit has some type of bodily form, such as a head, hands, feet, and so forth, as God, who is a spirit (John 4:24), is noted to have hands, feet, eyes, ears, and other features, like man, who was created in His image (Gen. 1:26–27).

With the written Word of God and the dynamic power and authority delegated to believers through the Holy Spirit, there may not be the need for angelic appearances in the form of men as there was prior to the church age. However, the invisible side of the angelic world is very much active and continues to do the work of the kingdom, especially during prophetic seasons.

The Greatest Season of Angels

In the entire Bible, there is no other single time frame in which more angelic resources are put into place than from the conception to the ascension of Christ—a time frame estimated as thirty-five years. In the four gospels, there are two very specific and detailed times recorded in the ministry of Christ, where God commissioned

angelic assistance to minister strength and encouragement to him: one at the beginning and the other at the
conclusion of his ministry.

After Christ's baptism in water, the Holy Spirit
directed Him into the Judean wilderness for a forty-
day mission of fasting and prayer. During the entire
forty days, Satan tempted Him. We read, "Then the
tempter came to Him and said to him..." (Luke 4:3).
The tempter is "the devil" or Satan (Luke 4:8, 10) who
is also an angel, a fallen cherub that directed a rebellion
against God. The question is: Was this temptation in the
form of *mental thoughts* that Satan shot in the form of
fiery darts (Eph. 6:16), or did Satan himself *appear visibly* to Christ and speak audibly to Him? The narrative
implies that the test was personally conducted by Satan
face-to-face, and Christ heard the voice of His arch-
enemy, as when the test concluded we read, "the devil
departed from him and the angels came and ministered
to him" (Luke 4:11).

At the end of forty days, Christ was at His weakest
physical moment. Matthew also noted that after the
devil left Him, "angels came and ministered unto him"
(Matt. 4:11). The word "ministered" here comes from
the same word used in the New Testament for a "dea-
con," a man in the church who attends to the needs of
others. It is a word indicating that the angels were caring
for the needs of Christ, which *may* have included providing food for Him. Christ's forty days in the Judean

wilderness was parallel to Israel's forty years in the Sinai desert, where food was unavailable and God provided manna, which is called "angel's food" (Ps. 78:25). After the forty days of testing, Christ "hungered," and there is no record of when or how He was fed after the temptation, as He immediately returned to Galilee (Luke 4:18), which would be several days' walking. Did the angels bring heavenly manna for Christ, in the same manner that God provided for Israel, or the same way deacons fed those in need in the early church (Acts 6:1–4)?

Fast-forward forty-two months, at the conclusion of Christ's public ministry. In John 14, Christ alludes to His upcoming prayer time in the Garden of Gethsemane. He informed His disciples: "I will no longer talk much with you, for the ruler of this world is coming and has nothing in me" (John 14:30 NKJV). The ruler of this world is Satan. In the garden, as Christ began interceding, His sweat became as great drops of blood (Luke 22:44). The Father was placing the sins of mankind upon His Son, as Paul indicates that "he hath made him to be sin for us, who knew no sin; that we might be made the righteousness of God in him" (2 Cor. 5:21).

This transfer of man's sins to Christ was a mystery hid from the foundation of the world and was unknown in the kingdom of Satan. Paul wrote that if the princes of this world would have known this redemption mystery, they would have "never crucified the Lord of glory" (1 Cor. 2:8). The ruler of this world, Satan, was present in the garden during Christ's extreme agony, and heard Christ's praying to the Father asking if it were possible for the "cup" (of suffering) to pass from Him. In this midst of emotional agony, Luke wrote, "And there appeared an angel unto him from heaven, strengthening him" (Luke 22:43).

Later, when Christ stood to be arrested, Peter suddenly sliced off the ear of Malchus, servant of the High Priest. Jesus healed the man and told Peter to put his sword away (John 18:10–11). Then Christ revealed this amazing fact: "Or do you think that I cannot now pray to My Father, and He will provide Me with more than twelve legions of angels?" (Matt. 26:53 NKJV).

Prior to this revelation in the garden, there is no mention of these legions of angelic deliverers. Why were there twelve legions? In 2 Kings 19:35, one angel walked through the army of Assyrians, slaying 185,000 in one night. In Christ's time, one Roman legion could be as many as 6,000 armed soldiers, making twelve legions as many as 72,000 angels. The number 12 is significant, as without Judas, there were 11 disciples, and with Christ, 12 persons were in the garden, implying that one legion could be assigned to each of the 12 men.

Since angels can bring revelation from God to earth, this angel appearing to Christ in the midst of His mental and emotion pain would have revealed to Him the *rescue option* provided as a backup plan should Christ choose to call off His Father's ultimate redemption plan, which prophetically included the scourging (Isa. 53:5) and the crucifixion (Ps. 22:16). Christ, however, rejected this optional plan and reminded Peter, "How then could the Scriptures be fulfilled, that this must happen?" (Matt. 26:54).

The ministry of the angels far exceeded the influence and authority of Satan, as the strength of Satan was diminished when the spoken Word of God (Heb. 4:12) cut through the voice of the adversary, and angels brought physical, emotional, and spiritual renewal to a weary Son, from His Heavenly Father. When angels ministered to Christ, they all appeared in the forms of men.

Angels appeared in human form at Christ's resurrection as well. In addition to the angel who rolled the stone away from the tomb (Matt. 28:3), Luke describes an encounter in which two men in shining clothes stood outside the tomb announcing Christ's resurrection to the women (Luke 24:4–5). Forty days later at Christ's ascension, "two men in white apparel said, 'This same Jesus which was taken up from you into heaven will so come in like manner as you have seen him go'" (Acts 1:11).

During His temptation in Luke 4, there was intense pressure on Christ's body (hunger), soul (mind), and spirit. The Garden of Gethsemane also affected all three aspects of the human nature: mind, body, and spirit. Satan was personally present during these two seasons of Christ's ministry as disobedience in either narrative and any wrong decision would have destroyed

Christ's purpose and mankind's destiny. Christ's weakness required supernatural intervention brought to Him by angels who carry with them the divine presence of God. Peter wrote that there is "refreshing" that comes from the presence of the Lord (Acts 3:19), and angels bring this refreshing.

CAN CERTAIN ANIMALS SENSE OR SEE ANGELS IF THEY ARE IN A ROOM?

This is an interesting question. We know from Scripture that humans have some type of a veil or covering over their eyes that prevents them from seeing all types of spirits, including angels. Only when this covering is lifted can a person see the invisible. When Elisha prayed, the eyes of his servant opened to see the chariots and horses of fire (2 Kings 6:15–17). Elisha himself was supernaturally able to see Elijah's angelic transportation to heaven, when the other fifty sons of the prophets standing at a distance saw nothing but a whirlwind (2 Kings 2). When Christ was raised from the grave, He appeared to two men with veiled eyes who did not recognize Him. Only when the veil was removed did they realize they were speaking to Christ (Luke 24:13–31).

It may be that this veil hiding the spirit world from human eyes is a part of our sin nature that was initiated at the fall. When Adam sinned, he could still hear the voice of God in the garden, but people would no longer see God face-to-face in fellowship (Gen. 3). When Adam and Eve sinned, a series of curses was initiated, but the only curse placed on the animal kingdom was upon the serpent, who was doomed "above all cattle and above every beast of the field" (Gen. 3:14). The animals, cattle, and other "beasts" had no sin nature and were therefore incapable of sinning.

This is important to note when Balaam rode his donkey to the top of a mountain in Moab to place a curse on Israel. The Lord instructed him not to go, but the seer rebelled and continued on his way. Moses wrote that God sent an angel to block Balaam's path. The oddity is that the donkey clearly saw the angel and Balaam saw nothing. The donkey refused to move forward (Numbers 22:23–27). Nowhere does the passage say that the Lord opened the eyes of the donkey to see the angel. This is the only place in Scripture where an animal visibly sees an angel, and apparently thinks a man is standing in his path.

This one verse in no way proves that when an angel is present, animals can sense it. However, there are too many stories to tell where certain animals inside a home can at times sense both a good and an evil presence within the home. Dogs have a keen sense of smell and also are able to sense fear, anger, and grief in their owners. There have been times when animals have acted in a peculiar manner, as though something is troubling them or they are sensing someone in the room. It is possible that, at times, some animals can sense the presence of angelic and even demonic spirits when they are present.

CHAPTER FOUR

ANGELS OF HEALING

There is a church tradition of an angel being assigned as God's healing angel, whose name is Raphael. The early church father Origen (c. AD 185–254) wrote of certain assignments of angels and named Raphael as doing "the work of curing and healing." The name "Raphael" is unique for numerous reasons. God Himself revealed to the Israelites that if they followed Him in full obedience, He would not allow any Egyptian diseases to come upon them. He also gave His people a covenant name that when spoken identified Him as their healer, as in "For I am the Lord that healeth thee" (Exod. 15:26). The Hebrew word for "healeth" is *raphe,* which means to mend something by stitching or, figuratively, to cure, heal, or make whole. The name "Raphael" conceals healing within his name, meaning "God heals." Raphael is considered (by tradition) to be one of the seven archangels in heaven, alongside Gabriel and Michael.

Raphael

Raphael is alluded to in all three monotheistic religions: Judaism, Christianity, and Islam. The basis for some of the traditions is found in the writings of the noncanonical book of Tobit, which is accepted in the Catholic Church as deuterocanonical. In the story, Tobit asks Raphael to heal his eyes and to deliver his future daughter-in-law from an evil spirit. In Judaism, in the book of Enoch, there are four archangels mentioned: Michael, Gabriel, Uriel, and Raphael, who allegedly assisted in binding the evil spirit Azazel under a desert mountain (Enoch 10:4–6).

The story of an angel bringing healing in John 5 caused some in the early church to connect the angel with Raphael:

Now there is in Jerusalem by the Sheep Gate a pool, which is called in Hebrew, Bethesda, having five porches. In these lay a great multitude of sick people, blind, lame, paralyzed, waiting for the moving of the water. For an angel went down at a certain time into the pool and stirred up the water; then whoever stepped in first, after the stirring of the water, was made well of whatever disease he had. (John 5:2–4)

John is the only gospel writer to record this fascinating story.

This angel "went down," which implies a special angel was sent "down" from heaven to this specific location for a single purpose: to bring healing to the first person who could discern the moving of the waters. This angel was commissioned to appear during a set time, or "season" (KJV). In Jewish thought, Israel's special "seasons" were the seven "festivals" of Israel, called in Hebrew the *moadim*, or "appointed times" (Lev. 23). Some theologians suggest that this angel was sent to Jerusalem during one of Israel's seven festivals, likely Passover. The theory of Passover is significant. First, all men over twenty were required to attend this festival in Jerusalem, where Christ was at this time. He was mostly seen during the festivals. Second, the greatest mass healing on record occurred the night the Hebrew people ate the lamb in their homes at the first Passover (Exod. 12:5–10). The Psalmist wrote that "God brought them forth...and not a feeble person was among them" (Ps. 105:37). The lamb's blood marking the outer doors protected the firstborns inside the home. However, by eating the pascal lamb, whatever infirmity or weakness was affecting their bodies was removed, resulting in an instant healing.

For the journey, the sick needed curing and the elderly needed strength. Therefore, Passover is both a redemptive and a healing festival. Apparently, the multitude of infirm and sick at the pool of Bethesda assembled, knowing the *season* when the healing angel would descend. There Christ healed a man, who church father Chrysostom suggested was blind, and therefore had difficulty seeing when the water was troubling. He could, however, hear the commotion of others moving once the water began stirring, but he was never able to move fast enough to be the first one in. His condition was some form of palsy, or part of his body was paralyzed, requiring others to assist him when he moved from one location to another, as indicated by, "No man assisted him by putting him into the water." After speaking to this man, Jesus said to him, " 'Rise, take up thy bed, and walk.' And immediately the man was made whole" (John 5:8-9).

An Angel During the Healing Revival

Throughout church history God has continued to perform miracles and heal the sick. God's healing covenant never ceased and, even in the twentieth-century seasons of healing, was released upon the Body of Christ. During this healing season, godly men and women often reported sensing the presence or a manifestation of an angel of the Lord prior to receiving healing.

Shortly after the reestablishment of Israel as a nation in May 1948, America entered a unique "season" of revival, which many full-gospel theologians identified as the "Restoration Revival" or the "Great Healing Revival." This revival continued strong for seven consecutive years

(1948–1955), peaking around 1955. During this season, tens of thousands of believers in North America witnessed astonishing miracles, while sitting in giant tent cathedrals and large auditoriums. Gifted and anointed ministers would lay their hands upon the sick, offering a prayer of faith, and the audience would immediately see answers, as many seekers received healing through the "gifts of healing" or the "gift of the working of miracles" (see 1 Cor. 12:9–10). Many noted men such as T. L. Lowery, Oral Roberts, Morris Cerullo, R. W. Shambach, and my own father, Fred Stone, entered the ministry during this era of awakening.

One of the most noted and, at times, controversial figures of the post-war healing revival, whose ministry extended from the 1940s until his death in the 1960s, was a minister named William Branham. Having met and fellowshipped with ministers over the years who personally knew and ministered with Branham, I have heard their amazing stories of the spiritual gift God imparted to Branham, a very humble man, to minister to the needs of the oppressed and the sick. In many cases, the miracles were so clear and dramatic that sinners came to believe in Christ. He was called upon to pray for kings in Europe and in South Africa; after a major healing campaign, there was a parade of seven cattle trucks loaded with canes, crutches, and wheelchairs and thousands of healed people singing "Only Believe."

The most unusual manifestation, and the most criticized by skeptics of Branham's ministry, was when an angel of the Lord that God assigned to his ministry would manifest during the public healing campaigns. He could discern the moment that the angelic messenger was present, and the results that followed his prayers—the stunning miracles—made it clear that the supernatural power of God was present to heal the people. Branham privately told close friends that when this angel was present in the auditorium, it would stand near the sick person and the area near them would illuminate. This was how he knew a healing miracle was coming. Just as an angel of the Lord appeared at the pool of Bethesda during a specific season, the miracles that followed were proof that the widely circulated story of a healing angel was true. Jesus said, "Believe me that I am in the Father, and the Father in me: or else believe me for the very works' sake" (John 14:11).

Supernatural Healing of My Father

When I was a small child, my father, Fred Stone, a pastor in Big Stone Gap, Virginia, was sent away to a hospital. I knew something was wrong at the time, but didn't learn the whole story until I was older. Dad had begun to feel pain under his heart, and his doctor diagnosed him with a tumor and referred him to University of Virginia Medical Center in Charlottesville for further tests. Dad shared the experience in his book *Fire on the Altar*:

On the sixth day, as I stood and looked out the window of my room on the fourth floor, I sensed that someone was watching me. I turned around but the other patient in the room was reading a newspaper, so I knew it wasn't him. When I turned back to look out the window, I saw a man outside standing in mid-air! I knew he had to be one of God's angels or some kind of manifestation of the Holy Spirit, because what human could be standing outside a fourth floor window in mid-air?

This man looked intently at me, from the top of my head down to my feet, as though he was examining me. Then he took a few steps and walked toward me. He had a spiritual body, and his body walked right through mine, and I actually felt my back to his. This lasted for a few seconds, then he stepped back through the window and once again faced me. He looked intently one more time before he turned and vanished. Immediately I felt energy from the top of my head to the bottom of my feet, and it was evident that God's supernatural power had touched my body. I left the room and walked down four flights of stairs to the lobby (which I could not do before). I walked around the lobby twice, and then I bolted up the same stairs to my room. When I got to the fourth floor I was not even out of breath.

When Dad returned to his room, he received a call from his brother-in-law, Frank Campbell, in Mentor, Ohio. Frank told him that at 8 o'clock that evening, his pastor had asked him if he had a brother in ministry who was sick. When Frank said yes, the pastor asked him to come forward and the congregation prayed on Dad's behalf—at the same time the man appeared outside Dad's window. This reminded me of how the church prayed steadfastly when Peter was arrested and was scheduled to be executed after Passover. The same exact time the church was in prayer, God sent an angel of deliverance to free Peter from the prison (see Acts 12:1–11).

When Dad told the doctors what had happened the next morning, they were skeptical. However, even after several more days of testing, no trace of the deep internal bleeding they had detected in previous tests could be found. Neither the tumor nor the bleeding ever returned. We discussed this miracle on several occasions and Dad would say, "The more I think about seeing what appeared to be a man that could move through a window, the more I believe this was a healing angel sent from the Lord."

Biblical Methods of Healing

Paul wrote: "And the very God of peace sanctify you wholly; and I pray God your whole spirit and soul and body be preserved blameless unto the coming of our Lord Jesus Christ" (1 Thess. 5:23). God desires us to be both *holy* and *whole* (Heb.12:14; 1 Thess. 5:23). The common New Testament Greek word for "whole" is *holos*, meaning "altogether." It alludes to being healthy in body, soul, and spirit or, as we would say today, totally healthy. The "whole" man consists of the body (physical), soul (emotional), and spirit (spiritual). A person who is physically strong yet emotionally unstable is not completely whole. Someone who is spiritually strong yet physically sick to the point they cannot function is not totally whole. It is the will of God to preserve (to keep strong) our tri-part being (body, soul, and spirit), preserved until the time our life is complete or until Christ returns—whichever comes first.

Using the Scripture as our guide, there are four New Testament (New Covenant) methods used to bring healing. While there are many Scriptures to back up each method, I will only mention one reference for each:

1. The method of laying on of hands (Mark 16:18)

Christ, His disciples, and the New Testament apostles would lay their hands upon the sick to impart healing. According to Mark 5:30, those who exercised faith could literally feel the healing "virtue" (power) enter their bodies (Mark 5:30). Numerous examples are found where the sick were cured through the ministry of laying on of hands. Laying on of hands is also a basic doctrine in the

Christian Church (Heb. 6:2). Using this method, certain spiritual gifts are also transferable (2 Tim. 1:6).

2. The method of the anointing with oil (James 5:14–15)

James instructed the elders in the church to anoint the sick with oil: "Is any sick among you? Let him call for the elders of the church; and let them pray over him, anointing him with oil in the name of the Lord: And the prayer of faith shall save the sick, and the Lord shall raise him up; and if he has committed sins, they shall be forgiven him."

Oil is a symbol of the anointing of the Holy Spirit. In the early church, the elders (the older and spiritually mature men in the congregation) would pray over the sick and anoint them with oil. If the prayer was offered "with faith," the sick would be healed. The healed person was then required to confess their faults one to another, and to pray for others.

3. The operation of the gifts of healing and working of miracles (1 Cor. 12:7–10)

A manifestation of the gifts of healing and working of miracles is found in 1 Corinthians 12:7–10: "For to one is given by the Spirit the word of wisdom; to another the word of knowledge by the same Spirit; to another faith by the same Spirit; to another the gifts of healing by the same Spirit. To another the working of miracles…" These gifts are a supernatural impartation from the Holy Spirit, providing the ability to pray for the sick and afflicted, releasing a manifestation of God's miraculous power. Throughout history, God has used the prayers of righteous men and women to experience miracles of answered prayer, including miracles of healing (James 5:16).

4. The power of the spoken Word (Ps. 107:20)

There are several New Testament examples where Christ simply spoke the word to bring healing to the infirm. A centurion had a sick servant at home and came to Christ, saying, "Speak the word only and my servant shall be healed" (Matt. 8:8). The man's servant was cured the very moment Christ spoke the healing word (Matt. 8:13). Jesus said this was the greatest level of faith, to have faith in the power of the spoken word (Matt. 8:10).

At times a person will stand in place on behalf of another person, as my dad's brother-in-law did. A prayer of faith is offered in the name of the Lord on behalf of the person who is suffering. This agrees with Psalms 107:20: "He sent his word, and healed them, and delivered them from their destructions." Based upon the John 5 narrative, we must add the possibility of God permitting an angel of healing to bring His healing power to a person in need of a miracle.

When asking for healing, we are to ask God in the name of the Lord Jesus Christ for His healing power to manifest in our mind, body, or spirit—wherever the healing is needed. Angels of healing are activated under the authority and commandment of the Lord and we should *never pray directly to any angel*. However, even if we do not need a physical healing, we can petition God to provide supernatural strength from angels, as part of their ministry is to strengthen those who are in spiritual battles. This passage in Daniel affirms this fact:

And suddenly, one having the likeness of the sons of men touched my lips; then I opened my mouth and spoke, saying to him who stood before me, "My lord, because of the vision my sorrows have overwhelmed me, and I have retained no strength. For how can this servant of my lord talk with you, my lord? As for me, no strength remains in me now, nor is any breath left in me." Then again, the one having the likeness of a man touched me and strengthened me. And he said, "O man greatly beloved, fear not! Peace be to you; be strong, yes, be strong!" So when he spoke to me I was strength- ened, and said, "Let my lord speak, for you have strengthened me." (Daniel 10:16–19 NKJV)

Angels continually dwell in God's presence; thus when they enter the earthly realm, the presence of God can be perceived if the believer is sensitive to spiritual atmo- spheres. Angels can and do strengthen us, and new cov- enant believers can ask the Lord to commission angels to assist us in strength and help us when needed.

WHY SHOULD WE NEVER PRAY DIRECTLY TO AN ANGEL?

The Bible instructs all believers how to pray, and in no Biblical instance did a person pray directly to an angel unless the "angel of the Lord" was the Lord Himself. Under the New Covenant, we are to petition the Heavenly Father using the authority of the name of Jesus Christ (John 16:23). Christ said to ask in His name and we would receive, that our joy may be full (John 16:24). Nowhere, and at no time from Adam to John the apostle, did a godly person pray in the name of some angel. From the time of Moses on, it was common for men to pray in the name of the God of "Abraham, Isaac, and Jacob" (Exod. 32:13; Lev. 26:42; Deut. 9:27; 1 Kings 18:36). In the New Testament, prayers are said in the name of Christ, including prayers for salvation (Acts 2:38) and healing (Acts 3:6; James 5:14), and all prayers were to be spoken in the name of Jesus Christ, as this was required to approach the throne of God.

This is perhaps the reason that only two angels are mentioned by name in Scripture: Gabriel and Michael (Luke 1:19; Rev. 12; Jude 9). There are older main-line churches that at times tend to bring attention to both of these angels. If the Lord mentioned all of the unnamed angels in Scripture, it is quite possible, knowing the nature of men, that some form of angelic worship would have emerged in the church. The name of Christ is the only name under heaven whereby man can be saved (Acts 4:12).

CHAPTER FIVE

ANGELS OF PROTECTION

In my childhood home, there was a picture hanging on the wall of two small children crossing a partially broken bridge and a beautiful angel (a motherly figure with a robe and wings) secretly protecting them as they crossed. It was my favorite picture and actually gave me comfort when I saw it, reminding me that God had an angel that was watching over me. This was important since I slept alone in a small room that often became cold (we used a small coal furnace).

Parents often speak of "guardian angels." While the phrase "guardian" is not found anywhere in the Scripture, if we carefully examine several key Biblical verses and narratives, there are powerful implications that God certainly does employ angelic supervision on behalf of children.

Angels Who Protect Children

Christ loved children and set aside time in His busy schedule to pray special blessings over them. Parents

would present their infants to Christ to lay His hands
upon them and bless them (Mark 10:13). Some of His
disciples viewed this as a distraction, even rebuking
the parents. Christ was displeased and told them not
to interfere with this important ministry. He reminded
them that the kingdom of heaven is made up of children (Mark 10:14). Christ would lift the children up
in His arms, put His hand upon them, and bless them
(Mark 10:16).

Christ gave an interesting revelation concerning
children in Matthew 18:10: "Take heed that ye despise
not one of these little ones; for I say unto you, that in
heaven their angels do always behold the face of my
Father which is in heaven." Christ was intent on making it clear that adults should be aware of how they treat
(or mistreat) a child, warning that it would be better to
tie a millstone (a large rock used for grinding grain)
around their neck and jump into the sea than to offend
a child (Matt. 18:6). Christ then revealed that angels
are assigned to children and continually see the face of
God in heaven. This verse brings up several interesting
points. God's love for children is so intense that a host of
angels who are continually before His throne is assigned
to them. But for which reasons?

There are several schools of thought. The context of
this verse is a warning about harming or offending a
child. Are these angels assigned by God to enact pun-
ishment in some form against those who are harming

children? Or are these angels commissioned by the Lord to go throughout the earth and oversee the protection and direction of children? Christ said "their angels," meaning children have personal angels who are with them.

One of my favorite passages that speaks of angels' protective assignments is penned in Psalms 34:7: "The angel of the LORD encampeth round about them that fear him, and delivereth them." The Hebrew word for "encampeth" actually alludes to a person pitching a tent with the idea of camping out on a piece of property. One good example is with Job, a wealthy man whom Satan targeted. Satan confessed that a special "hedge" surrounded Job, his property, and his family. Both God and Satan could see the invisible hedge that Job couldn't. Once the hedge was removed, Satan was given limited liberty to attack Job's family, finances, and health. The "hedge" was likely a group of angels that restrained any Satanic forces from entering the property of this godly man.

My father, Fred Stone, was one of the greatest intercessors I have ever known. It was common for him to pray for one hour every day, and when he was ministering at night, he would pray for several hours while meditating on the Word. I heard my dad pray a specific prayer over the family, especially his four children, for many years. It went like this: "Father, I ask you to protect my children [he would name each one] and keep them from harm, danger, and disabling accidents."

During my lifetime, I was in several car accidents and came out with no injuries. Years ago, while flying in my ministry plane, the right side of our twin-engine failed and we landed without injury. During another close call, I was exploring the top of an extinct volcano at Crater Lake, Oregon, when I suddenly fell and slid down the steep slope, digging my fingers into the hard dirt; yet I made it to the bottom only sore and dusty, without any injury. In each of these situations, prayer was offered before the event unfolded. Dad continually and earnestly prayed for angelic protection to surround the family and me.

Angels Are Given "Charge"

Psalms 91 deals with God protecting His people to ensure they have long, prosperous lives, and some Jewish Talmudists believe it was written by Moses in the wilderness after the plague of the fiery serpents, after which Israel was more humble and submissive to God.

It is a Psalm of protection from danger and in times of war, as noted with these words: "[God] shall deliver you from the snare of the fowler, and from the noisome pestilence...His truth shall be your shield and buckler...you will not be afraid of the terror by night nor the arrow that flies in the day. A thousand shall fall by your side and ten thousand by your right hand, but it will not come near to you" (Ps. 91:3–7). Verses 11–12 are also interesting: "For

He shall give His angels charge over you, to keep you in all your ways. In their hands they shall bear you up, lest you dash your foot against a stone" (NKJV).

The word "charge" here in Hebrew is *sha'al* and refers to placing a demand on someone to do something. In the New Testament when Paul "charged" Timothy, it suggests the military term for when a higher-ranking officer gives a command to a lower-ranking officer (1 Tim. 1:18). In this Psalm, God is speaking as the commander, oversee-ing all of His angelic hosts and placing a military-type instruction for the angels to protect His people. The Hebrew word for "keep" in Psalms 91 is *shamar*, and is the same word used in the daily blessing of the High Priest spoken over Israel, which reads, "The Lord bless and keep you…" (Num. 6:24). This word means to "hedge in; to guard and to protect." It is a powerful promise indicat-ing that God directly appoints angels to guard and hedge in His people. Notice the angel is to "bear you up." This Hebrew word for "bear" is *nasa'*, meaning to "lift up," and carries a variety of applications in Hebrew throughout the Old Testament. In many instances, it literally or figu-ratively refers to carrying something, including a person bearing their own iniquities (Lev. 20:19–20). The impli-cation is that angels would *lift a person up* to prevent them from falling into harm.

It should be noted that the sentence did not say "in their wings they will bear you up," but "in their hands." The Hebrew word for "hands" is *kaph*, and refers to the "hollow" of the hand. The eleventh letter of the Hebrew alphabet is *kaf*, or *khaf*, and the symbol representing this letter is the palm of the hand. In Scripture, some angels are identified as having wings and others hands, and some both, as indicated when Ezekiel described the Cherub whose hands were under their wings: "And they had the hands of a man under their wings on their four sides; and they four had their faces and their wings" (Ezek. 1:8 KJV).

Isaiah describes seraphim, a unique worshipping angel, as having six wings (Isa. 6:1–2), two of which are used for flying. Zechariah saw a vision of two angels with wings like storks (Zech. 5:9) that were used to carry various items; in this case, a woman in a lead basket. Solomon also penned an unusual proverb in Ecclesiastes 10:20: "Curse not the king, no not in thy thought; and curse not the rich in thy bedchamber: for a bird of the air shall carry the voice, and that which hath wings shall tell the matter."

Some suggest the "bird" here would be a carrier pigeon, as they were used to send messages from the private rooms of the kings and wealthy individuals to faraway locations. However, there may be another application, concealed in this verse. That which "hath wings" in the natural realm would be the fowl or birds of the air. In the spirit realm, however, angels can listen in on secret conversations and report the information to other angels. This is what transpired when the Syrian king secretly planned an invasion of Israel, and twice

Elisha the prophet warned the king of Israel to move his troops, in attempts to prevent the ambush. When the King of Syria demanded to know who in his army was secretly spying for Israel, a soldier spoke up, saying, "None, my lord, O king; but Elisha, the prophet who is in Israel, tells the king of Israel the words that you speak in your bedroom" (2 Kings 6:2 NKJV).

This secret military attack spoken of in the Syrian king's bedchamber was made known by the Lord to Elisha, who was living in Israel. Angels were certainly involved in this scenario, as proven when the Syrian king led his army to Dothan to capture Elisha. Unknown by the king, God had sent angelic horses and chariots of fire to surround the city and protect Elisha from any harm (2 Kings 6:14–16).

The Scripture is replete with verses and narratives indicating God's willingness to commission angels to protect His people from harm and danger. Some Christians prefer not to use the term "guardian angel," as the phrase is missing from Scripture. However, the phrase is an accurate term to identify the assignment of any angel, "given charge to bear up" a child of God.

Applying Protective Principles

Throughout the Old Testament there are what theologians call "types and shadows." A type (from the Greek word *typos*) is an event, person, or narrative in the history of Israel that is a preview of the redemptive work of Christ in the New Testament. The Old Testament is the shadow, but the reality is Christ. For example, the lamb offered at Passover is a "type" of Christ—the Lamb of God who was crucified at the time of Passover.

There are in the Old Testament numerous spiritual principles that have an application under the New Covenant. For example, the High Priest daily blessed the people with a specific prayer of favor and blessing. Christ taught His disciples to pray and ask God for His daily provision. In the tabernacle and Temple, in the morning and the evening, a lamb was offered each day. Thus blood was applied twice daily. The blood of Christ is applied by the confession of our mouth as we "overcome Satan by the blood of the lamb and by the word of our testimony" (Rev. 12:11). Just as the sacrifices were made at the beginning and ending of each day, I have taught the principle that parents should pray a protective hedge over their children in the morning before they walk out of their home and in the evening before they go to bed. This hedge is formed by confessing the blood of Christ over their bodies, souls, and spirits.

In what we call "The Lord's Prayer," Christ said we should pray that God would "deliver us from evil" (Matt. 6:13). In Greek, this can be read as "deliver us from the wicked one." Satan is called "the wicked (evil) one." It is noted that the phrase "deliver us" has been translated by older scholars as to mean "break our chains," or the strongholds Satan exercises over us, as deliverance from Satan requires breaking the yokes and bondages (Isa. 10:27).

As for protective angels, there are two ways they are released into a situation. One is by the sovereign will of God, in which He directs the assignment to fulfill His perfect will. The other is when prayer intercedes as believers ask God for that assistance. Why does it require us asking or praying, and why doesn't God just send angels without our asking? This would be like asking: Why doesn't God just save people from sin without asking, or heal the sick without them believing God is able, or fill people with the Spirit automatically without asking for it? The simple answer is there is a law of the Spirit and the Word that says God at times will do nothing until He is asked, as asking requires faith. The law of answered prayer works on the law of faith: asking and believing before receiving. Asking also demonstrates our dependency on God instead of our own ability.

We do what we can and God does what we cannot. Remember, when the enemy has a plan, prayer is what can restrain it from being initiated. Jesus warned Peter that Satan desired to "sift him as wheat." Then Jesus said, "But I have prayed for you that your faith will not fail" (Luke 22:31–32). Never minimize the effective prayers of a righteous person to prevent the strategy of Satan from coming to pass, and never underestimate the ability of the angels of God to protect you from danger, "for the angel of the Lord encamps around all those that fear Him and delivers them" (Ps. 34:7).

Protection comes through the promises of God's word that He is with us always, and will never leave us or forsake us (Heb. 13:5), and that His angels will encamp around us and deliver us (Ps. 34:7). Our part is to verbally confess God's Word out loud and to pray for hedges of protection using the name of Christ and apply by faith His protective blood. If the blood of earthly lambs could prevent the death angel from entering the Hebrew homes during the Exodus, then the word of our testimony and faith in the blood of Christ can form protective hedges.

We should also pray to the Heavenly Father, petitioning Him to commission His angels to be given charge of all of our bloodline, including infants and children.

IF WE HAVE ASKED GOD TO SEND ANGELS TO PROTECT OUR CHILDREN, HOW DO WE KNOW THEY ARE DOING IT?

This is where faith and trust play a role. There are numerous promises in Scripture that say if we ask anything according to God's will, He hears us (1 John 5:14). The will of God is seen in the verse "The angel of the Lord encamps around about those that fear the Lord and delivers them" (Ps. 34:7). Christ taught that if we ask the Father anything in His name, He will do it (John 14:14), and when we ask, we must believe it before we receive it (Mark 11:24). We cannot ask in faith and the next day speak unbelief. In my life, I know God has heard me when I can rest in peace and leave things in His hands.

However, I never ignore a burden of danger when I sense it. I will break away from my routine to pray in advance. Recently, I was burdened for six days with knowing someone was going to pass away in a certain family, despite no member being sick, and no other evidence the death could or would occur. I told the family that it would occur while they were in Israel on a tour. Near the conclusion of their trip, they received a phone call from a relative who said they were close to dying. I did not have any inclination to pray for an angel, but I believe the Lord allowed me to sense this to prepare them for what occurred.

At times, when praying, divine intervention occurs. When we ask God for angelic protection over our loved ones, we must believe He has heard us and believe the Covenant promise. When Jesus and his disciples were on a boat in the middle of a lake and He said, "Let us go over to the other side," a storm hit and the boat filled with water; yet Jesus was asleep in the hull. The disciples were fearful because they forgot the promise that said the "other side." Jesus was not afraid because he knew the storm would not sink the boat—so he slept. Confidence in God's promises will cause us to enter into a "rest" in our spirit.

CHAPTER SIX

ANGELS OF SALVATION

If you are actively serving Christ and know your name is written in heaven, your greatest burden on earth is to see your unsaved family members repent, turn to Christ, and receive a redemptive covenant of eternal life through Him. For many years I have pondered, outside of prayer, witnessing, and laying claim to a promise of family salvation (Acts 16:31), is there any other spiritual resource we can tap into to assist in reaching our unconverted family members?

It is important to note that, in the New Testament, multitudes were won to Christ after hearing a clear explanation of proving He was the Messiah, either using the Scripture or through a dramatic healing miracle. Today, when a miracle occurs, there is much skepticism—especially in the West—and with various Biblical interpretations, some sinners are more confused as churches argue doctrine instead of presenting Christ as our Savior!

Angelic Assistance

Perhaps there is a source that we should tap into: asking God for angelic assistance in reaching our family. Hebrews 1:14 speaks of angels, and there are several different Bible translations and word studies:

- "Are they not all ministering spirits, sent forth to minister for them who shall be heirs of salvation?" (KJV)
- "Are they not all ministering spirits sent forth to minister for those who will inherit salvation?" (NKJV)
- "Are not the angels all ministering spirits (servants) sent out in the service [of God for the assistance] of those who are to inherit salvation?" (AMP)

If the interpretation I will present is correct, then there is a great promise of how God's attention is turned toward not only saving your lost family members, but assigning angels to assist in the process.

Either Paul or Titus penned the book of Hebrews, or as others believe, a scribe appointed by Paul assisted in dictating the content of this fabulous epistle. It was addressed to the Hebrew (Jewish) believers who had received Christ as their Messiah and were being persecuted for their beliefs. Some out of fear were returning to the rituals at the Temple, which Paul taught were no longer valid to forgive sins (Heb. 6:4–6).

In Hebrews 1, Paul alludes to angels in six of fourteen verses (Heb. 1:4–7, 13–14). His emphasis is that Christ is far better than the angels (Heb. 1:4), and the writer emphasizes that they are spirits (Heb. 1:7). Christians often hear Hebrews 1:14 quoted to indicate that angels are assigned to minister to us as believers, since we are the "heirs of salvation." We are presently "heirs with God and joint heirs with Jesus Christ" (Rom. 8:17). However, in the wording of this verse, the angelic ministry is for those who "shall be heirs," "who will inherit," and "are to inherit."

Paul was formerly Saul of Tarsus, a strict law-observing Pharisee whose mind was set on destroying the new sect that was following the man from Nazareth. Without his knowledge, Saul was marked in his mother's womb by the Lord to be an apostle. He wrote: "But when it pleased God, who separated me from my mother's womb, and called me by His grace…" (Gal. 1:15). In order to reach Saul and break the religious spirit that gripped him, God paid him a supernatural visit on the road to Damascus, where a blinding light came and a voice from heaven spoke to him (Acts 9:3–4). Later in Paul's ministry there were angels connected with his ministry who appeared at times to give him instruction (Acts 27:23).

We know that one of the primary duties of the Holy Spirit is to convict men of sin, then point them to Christ

(John 16:8). A sinner cannot be drawn to the Heavenly Father unless the Holy Spirit pulls them. However, it has been my observation, after forty-two years of ministry, that the majority of sinners who turn to Christ are influenced by a person they know—either a family member, a coworker, or a friend they admire and trust.

Many years ago, a noted minister who was traveling throughout the United States had a daughter who was heavily addicted to drugs, and living a wild lifestyle with no interest in following Christ. In fact, at times she would mock her father by pointing out that he was traveling the nation and winning others but was having no impact on her life. Without her knowledge, her father had been intently praying that God would send an angel to visit her and this would cause her to turn her life around. He believed that, for his daughter to be delivered, it required a supernatural manifestation to seize her attention.

One night when the pastor was back home, his daughter came in late, and he heard a scream coming from her room. She ran to him and said, "Dad, he is in my room and scaring me!"

He asked who was in her room and she replied, "It's an angel, Dad, and he's really big! I'm scared!"

Her dad calmly replied, "I'm glad he showed up. I've been praying for you to see him for a long time!" The encounter did lead to her deliverance from addiction, and she followed the Lord faithfully, until she went home to heaven.

Just as an angel of the Lord connected the apostle Peter and Cornelius, the Italian Roman centurion—two men that had never met—for the purpose of Gentiles being grafted into the New Covenant, angels can and *do* bring people together, often via a believer who can lead an unbeliever to Christ.

Following the Still Small Voice

Angels are not assigned to initiate conviction of sin in the heart of a sinner, as this is the responsibility of the Holy Spirit. When a message is preached to the lost, the Holy Spirit activates the need for salvation in the heart of the hearer. The Holy Spirit is always pointing individuals to Christ, as Jesus noted, "He [*the Spirit*] will not speak of himself" (John 16:13), and he will "reprove [*convict to convince*] the world of sin…" (John 16:8; italics mine). An angel's limitation is the inability to be omnipresent—a quality given to the Holy Spirit.

Angels, however, do consistently operate behind the scenes to connect people together for significant purposes. For example, in the past I have experienced a sudden nudge to leave my office and drive through an area without knowing why, only to end up in some restaurant or business. Moments later I would encounter someone who needed encouragement, or was praying for a special blessing. I have walked into stores and felt that the employee behind the counter needed money for a specific purpose. After I handed the strangers money, they confessed they had just prayed for gas money or added income, and the Lord led me their way as an answer to their prayer.

Years ago, I flew to Orange County, California, to minister at Free Chapel Worship Center. Before the service began that day, I needed some nourishment. As we discussed a place to eat, just outside the hotel I saw a restaurant and was actually "pulled in my spirit" to the place. I learned years ago not to resist those unusual burdens and strange "nudges" that suddenly press into my spirit at unexpected moments. The place was packed and we waited at the front for a table. Suddenly, through the door walked a well-known NBA basketball star. The woman seating us said, "There is a table near the bar and it's the only one available at this time." Since I do not drink alcohol and am a minister conscious of perceptions, I was hesitant but said, "Okay, I'm in a hurry." Oddly, it was the right place, as moments later, the NBA player came over, pulled up a chair at my table, and we began talking. I knew then that the Lord, through an angel pressing on me and directing my path, had led me to witness to him.

While sitting at the table, I received a word of knowledge that the player's mother's prayers had come up before God and the Lord wanted him to follow Him. He looked stunned, as I knew nothing about him or his mother. He then told me his mom had passed away, and had played the organ at a church for sixty years and she had raised him there. I told him prayers are stored in heaven (Rev. 5:8), the prayer vial of his mother was coming before God, and I was talking to him to confirm that. I proceeded to give him some bad news: that he would lose most of his wealth and he should turn to God, repent, and serve Him. The player grew angry, and he called me a "Bible thumper." I continued to give him the Word of the Lord, and when I left, I said, "You may never remember me, but remember what I said. It is coming." Weeks later, the news reported how he had lost most of his wealth, and was headed to a rehab facility to get help.

The Holy Spirit directed me that day, as I am filled with the Spirit and can discern the voice of the Lord. However, why and how did this well-known NBA star choose the same restaurant where I was, at the exact time, and find a table in an area where I would normally never sit? He was unsaved, but because his Christian mother had passed, her prayers were stored in the vials of heaven, and not forgotten. Not only had his mother prayed for him for years, but I later discovered he had a Christian sister who had done the same. I believe the Lord sent an angel to whisper in his ear the idea of going to that specific location at that time, without his knowledge of what was occurring.

It was an angel who gave Cornelius the name of Peter, and told him where he was and what he was to do (Acts 10:1–8). The Holy Spirit can work in the spirit of a believer and give them inspired ideas and thoughts, and direct them accordingly. However, since an unsaved person is not led by the Spirit or listening to the voice of the Lord, an angel's thoughts can be whispered in their ears to direct them in the path of the righteous. From there, the Holy Spirit can take charge.

Chased by an Angel

When David was in great distress, he wrote about the numerous enemies that surrounded him seeking his demise. He asked God, "Let them be as chaff in the wind and let the angel of the Lord chase them" (Ps. 35:5). In this narrative, David needed the Lord to "chase" or "drive away" his enemies, and was asking for divine assistance in this situation. At times, an angel may be needed to prevent a life-threatening accident in the life of someone who is actually not in covenant with God. How can we pray and what can we do when a person we love is away from Christ, without the redemptive covenant, and are in danger?

When God was set to scorch the wicked city of Sodom off the face of the earth, the Lord sent two angels to Sodom to assist in Lot's rescue from the destruction because Abraham, Lot's uncle, had a covenant with God (see Gen. 19). This wasn't because of Lot's relationship with Him but because of Abraham's covenant. Without Abraham's intervention, the entire population, including Lot and his daughters, would have perished.

When my son was horribly addicted to drugs and alcohol for about nine years, my wife, Pam, and I prayed continually that the powers of darkness would have "no power to take his life." I based my prayer on Satan attacking Job and assaulting his body with painful sores, but then God said to Satan, "You cannot take his life" (Job 2:6). God limited the influence of the attack to temporary physical pain only, and did not allow Job to encounter a premature death. Because of my son's rebellious actions, some suggested I "remove him from the house." I refused, as I knew that the "serpents" and the "wolves" (wicked people) would attempt to devour him, capitalizing on his addiction.

I replied, "As long as he is in my house, he is under my hedge, and the protective angel assigned in our family lineage will protect him because we are in covenant with God." I spent many hours during those nine years asking the angel to extend God's mercy, despite my son's danger-ous actions. I recalled what God said to Noah after the flood: "For the imagination of a man's heart is evil from his youth" (Gen. 8:21). There were two occasions in which death stalked my son and in both instances the angel of the Lord won the battle. This miracle was not just because of *our* prayers, but the combined prayers of many friends and ministry partners. I boldly asked the Lord to send His angels to keep the hedge of protection around my son for the sake of the covenant and for his future purpose.

Minister Kelvin McDaniel shared a powerful story from when he traveled to Indonesia, the world's largest Muslim majority nation, to preach. Some of the people did not like what he preached, and the next morning, two very angry men came in a truck and began pouring gasoline onto the ground of the church. The pastor said he, his wife, and several church members gathered and began crying out to God. When one of the men tried to light a match, it wouldn't catch. He continued many times with no success. As the people prayed, the pastor tried to talk the man into not burning down the church. The man looked up, shrieked, turned suddenly, and ran away screaming. Two young church members chased him, tackled him, and held him to the ground as he screamed, "Don't let him kill me! Don't let him kill me!"

The pastor told Kelvin, "I couldn't figure out what he was talking about. The man looked like he was fighting for his life. I yelled and said, 'No one is going to kill you,' but the man kept screaming, 'He's going to kill me! He's going to kill me!' I asked him, 'Who is going to kill you?' And he said, 'The angel!' "

The pastor later learned that when the man tried unsuccessfully to light the last match, he looked up at the church and an angel appeared to him. This angel called his name and said, "I am the angel of the Most High God, the one living God, the God of the Bible that this man is preaching. This is God's property and you are trying to burn down holy land. Your life is in danger for being here. Because your heart is not fixed on God, you will die this night if you touch this property."

This man had been running for his life before he

was stopped. As he was lying on the ground, he began repenting and saying, "I believe. I believe!" About thirty minutes passed before the man was able to get up from the ground. The pastor told him about Christ and the man gave his heart to the Lord.

The next morning, Kelvin was at the airport waiting for his flight home when he received a call from the pastor. He told Kelvin the man who tried to burn the church down had been converted the night before and was preaching to people from the roof of his house at that very moment. And people were stopping to listen, because it was such an unusual sight.

CAN ANGELS AT TIMES APPEAR TO LOOK LIKE OUR FAMILY MEMBERS?

There have been numerous accounts from people who believed they encountered an angel that had a very similar appearance to a person they were close to in this life. In some instances, the images were part of a vision a believer experienced. It is unclear from Scripture how or why an angel would take on a certain physical likeness, but we do know that nothing is impossible with God.

Angels can appear and be fearful to look upon to some. Samson's mother saw an angel and described it as "very terrible" (Judg. 13:6) or, as some translate, "very awesome" to look upon (Judg. 13:6). The actual Hebrew word used here translated as "terrible" is *yare'* and can mean "to frighten" or "frightening." Perhaps the Lord sends angels, whether in dreams or visions, to a person in a similar appearance to a loved one in order to bring peace and comfort.

CHAPTER SEVEN

ANGELS AT DEATH

There is a fascination some individuals have with death; not in the sense of experiencing it themselves, but a curiosity with what occurs when a person passes from this life. Their questions include: Is there a soul and spirit within the body? Is there an afterlife? If so, then how are the soul and spirit transported from the earthly realm to the eternal dimension where time is meaningless and the spirits of righteous men and woman dwell (Heb. 12:23)?

The Levels of Heaven

Biblical research indicates that heavenly space is divided into three dimensions, one layer sitting above the other. The first heaven is the level of Man's dominion, which consists of the air we breathe, the clouds that create rain, and the wind that blows. This is the heaven of the birds and what we call the "sky."

The second heaven surrounds the earth in all directions and is identified with the darkness that begins once a craft leaves the earth's atmosphere. The area of the sun, moon, and stars is called "heaven" in the Bible. The word "heaven" in Hebrew is *shamayim*, and includes both the level where the clouds produce water (*mayim*) and the celestial level of the sun, moon, and stars. This second region is immeasurable and it is impossible to find the edge of the galaxy, at least in this time. Scholars believe that this section of the upper world is where the spirit rebels Paul alluded to in Ephesians 6:12 exercise their dominion.

Our interest is the third level, or the third heaven. This is the highest level mentioned in the Scriptures, although there are extra-Biblical writings (such as the book of Enoch) that attempt to identify seven divisions of heaven, each with a specific characteristic. The idea may have stemmed from the early knowledge that there were seven planets spotted in the sky (including the sun and moon) and each had its own sphere or rule. The books of 1 and 3 Enoch have strange details of the cosmos that incorporate the belief that the second heaven is the dominion of fallen angels and satanic evil spirits, and the third heaven is the paradise of God. Without delving into a noncanonical book, the inspired apostle Paul relates that paradise (the abode of righteous souls) is in the third heaven.

When Paul was stoned in Lystra, he had either a

vision or an out-of-body experience in which he entered the heavenly paradise, the abode of righteous souls whose bodies are dust of the earth, but whose spirits were transported to a beautiful garden in heaven, to await the resurrection of the dead. Paul said:

> "I know a man in Christ who fourteen years ago—whether in the body I do not know, or whether out of the body I do not know, God knows—such a one was caught up to the third heaven. And I know such a man—whether in the body or out of the body I do not know, God knows—how he was caught up into Paradise and heard inexpressible words, which it is not lawful for a man to utter." (2 Corinthians 12:2–4 NKJV)

When Paul says he "knew a man," he is speaking of himself. The time frame, fourteen years prior, fits with when he was stoned and left for dead, and his alternative account in the city of Lystra (compare Acts 14:19–20 with 2 Cor. 12:2–4). We are never told whether or not he actually died. He says, "In the body I cannot tell or out of the body I cannot tell." The phrase "in the body" refers to a vision—a full-color three-dimensional visual image that occurs supernaturally. The term "out of the body" means the spirit is released from the body and travels to a specific location. Paul may have actually died, experienced a "life after death" manifestation, and through prayer was raised from the dead. Perhaps some of the revelation he later wrote concerning death and the judgment may have been from knowledge he'd gained in this amazing experience.

The Speed of Angels

From a purely rational perspective, human reasoning has difficulty comprehending angelic-spirit transportation that could thrust a person through a universe of stars and nebulas, faster than the speed of light. How can the soul and spirit of a departed family member make its way from Earth to the upper celestial world within seconds instead of millions of years?

The only immeasurable form of time travel that can theoretically move faster than light would be the "speed of thought." This is a dimension of movement that men have not yet measured. Many ministers believe this may be how angels travel. A spirit being has no physical limitation, and to move through the universe—which is millions of light-years in distance—a faster form of travel is required. An angel or a spirit can "think" themselves from one dimension to another via speed of thought. In this way, distance no longer matters, as the thought process cannot be measured as a length.

God is a spirit (John 4:24), angels are spirits (Heb. 1:7), and each living human has a body, soul, and spirit (1 Thess. 5:23). God as a spirit can be omnipresent, or in all places at the same time. This is not true with angels or humans. Angels in spirit form move as fast as lightning (Ezek. 1:13–14), and heavenly beings, when manifesting on earth, often appear in forms of light or brightness (Ezek. 10:4; Hab. 3:4; Acts 26:13). Angels can be in only one place at a time, yet they can travel faster than the speed of light because they are spirits. Each human in bodily form can be in only one physical location at a time until the moment they die and their spirit departs from their body, which can pass through solid objects (John 20:26) and transport from place to place using the speed of thought.

If you had literally stood in the third heaven as Paul did, then your mind could travel to faraway places you had visited or seen, and imagine what it would be like to return to that place, although your body limits the place to where you are. At death, if you have received Christ as your savior, then angels, being from paradise, can instantly move from their heavenly location to earth to release your spirit, which then enables you to time-travel at the same speed as angels.

Angels can "spirit travel" at will since their bodies are of a higher dimension than humans. Once an angel is commissioned to release the eternal spirit of a departed believer to paradise and travel from the earth zone back to the third heaven paradise zone, neither is limited by time or space, as both angels and the spirits of the righteous dead have a mysterious molecular structure that enables them to move at incredible speed without harm.

Just as the presence of God can be "felt" and the Holy
Spirit shifts an atmosphere during a service, the pres-
ence of angels can be felt if a person is in covenant with
God and they are keen to discern an angelic presence.
Both angels and departed spirits are invisible to the
human eye, but can be seen by all other forms of spirits.

Only when—and if—the veil is removed from the
human eyes can they see into the higher dimension of
the angelic world, as found in the story of Elisha. He
arose one morning and immediately saw horses and
chariots of fire surrounding the base of the mountain
where he lived, but his servant saw only the Syrian army.
That was until Elisha prayed for his servant's eyes to be
opened. Suddenly the invisible became visible and the
servant, too, saw God's supernatural army of protection (2 Kings 6:14–17). Paul taught that we would all be
known as we were known, meaning we will recognize
those in heaven if we knew them on earth (1 Cor. 13:12).

Many believers who have their eyes closed on the brink
of death will open them one last time and turn their
heads to an empty space in a room, or with a feeble hand
point in a certain direction. Those who can speak will
begin recognizing family members who passed before
them and describe them to be in the room. Doctors say
this occurs when the brain releases chemicals that create
hallucinations of departed family members. If this were
true, then everyone dying should experience similar
manifestations, yet they do not. It is also interesting to

note that I have never heard one story of a dying unsaved person who saw their loved ones welcoming them. To the contrary, unsaved and unrepentant people, if they are alert, often say they can feel fire moving in their feet and up their legs, and some began screaming to "get them off of me," and describe strange visions. These manifestations certainly do not occur every time, but there are countless eyewitness accounts where those who were present at the death sensed otherworldly presences in the room, or testify of their loved ones.

The Angel of Death

This brings us to the angel of death. In the medical field, a person is pronounced dead when the heart no longer beats and brain activity stops. Death in Scripture, however, is much more than the ceasing of bodily functions. Death is a separation of the eternal from the mortal, of the never-ending soul and spirit from the corruptible flesh of a person. The spirit must depart from the body and travel to its eternal destination, before the person on earth is dead.

The phrase "death angel," or "angel of death," is not found in the Bible. However, John describes in Revelation 6:8 seeing a horse and rider he identifies as "death and hell." This is not just an apocalyptic symbol, or a metaphor, as noted when reading Revelation 20:14: "And death and hell were cast into the lake of fire..."

You cannot cast a "symbol" or a "metaphor" into the lake of fire; thus, death and hell are spirits.

One of the most intriguing narratives is found in Exodus when God said, "I will pass through the land of Egypt this night and smite the firstborn in the land of Egypt..." (Exod. 12:12). Later we read, "At midnight, the Lord smote all the firstborn in the land of Egypt..." (Exod. 12:29). There was, however, another supernatural being involved the night of the Passover called the destroyer, the spirit that entered the home and took the life of the firstborn child. God instructed Israel to place the blood of the lamb on three spots of the outer doors of their homes, as it would protect their firstborn from death.

Death itself was introduced to man through the sin failure of Adam and Eve. Without access to the Tree of Life, Adam, Eve, and all of their descendants would eventually die. Satan is a literal fallen angel, hell has a spirit controlling it, and death is also a spirit. Death is an "enemy" of God and will be the last enemy destroyed (1 Cor. 15:26).

In the case of Elijah, 2 Kings narrates how the prophet was carried into heaven "alive," riding a chariot of fire pulled by spirit "horses of fire" (2 Kings 2:11). Notice there were no angels with him in the chariot. Angels appear at death, as they are responsible for separating the spirit from the body of the righteous and transporting it to the heavenly paradise. Elijah was not dead or dying; thus the heavenly chariot assisted in some form to move his human body through the cosmos at high and immeasurable speeds, bringing the prophet safely to God's presence, where he will reappear on earth as one of the two witnesses during the first part of the future great tribulation (Mal. 4:5; Rev. 11:3–6).

Christ gave us a powerful true story that reveals what occurs with a righteous and an unrighteous person at the moment of death, recorded in Luke 16:19–31. In the story, a beggar was lying at a rich man's gate, where the dogs were his only friends, licking the sores on his body. The beggar simply asked for crumbs from the table, but the rich man refused to feed this man and ignored his plea. The narrative reveals that both men died near the same time.

The rich man, after he passed with a full stomach "in hell he lifted up his eyes being in torments" and was tortured in the flame (Luke 16:23). When the beggar named Lazarus died starving, we read that he "was carried by the angels into Abraham's bosom..." (Luke 16:22). Abraham's bosom is believed to have been a massive subterranean chamber where all of the spirits of righteous saints were assigned, during what we call the Old Testament dispensation, upon their death.

Christ noted that "angels" (plural) and not a single "angel" assisted in the transporting of the soul and spirit of the beggar to his final dwelling place. There have been countless godly men and women who have experienced a near-death or a life-after-death experience. Many describe how men in bright clothes were in the room at the moment they departed. Some were revived and returned to tell their story.

Hebrews 9:27 explains that, "It is appointed unto men once to die and after this the judgment." We all have reservations about death, should we not go in the rapture of the church. Paul on several occasions thought his death was imminent and even accepted the possibility that he could depart (Acts 21:13). However, it was not God's *set time* or appointed time. I like what Daniel said when he wrote, "For at the time appointed the end shall be" (Dan. 8:19). Your end can only come by a divine appointment, considering Satan no longer carries the keys (authority) of death and hell. Your departure appointment is on God's calendar and not Satan's (Rev. 1:8).

In his final days in Rome, Paul was sentenced to execution. He wrote, "For I am now ready to be offered, and the time of my departure is at hand" (2 Tim. 4:6). The departure here was Paul's soul and spirit going to heaven after his death. Paul had written that when he was absent from the body, he would be present with the Lord (2 Cor. 5:8). At death, the soul and spirit are separated from the body; thus we depart this life and enter paradise in the third heaven (2 Cor. 12:1–4).

We must never accept a premature departure. Solomon pondered the question "Why should you die before the time?" (Eccl. 7:17). At times when we know someone is in danger of a premature departure, we should be as the church was in the time when Peter was scheduled for execution. They prayed continually, until the angel of the Lord released him from prison (Acts 12:4–16).

The Dead Saints Are Not Angels

One of the common misconceptions concerning the deceased righteous is that once their human spirit departs its physical body and is escorted by heavenly angels to paradise, they become angels themselves. This unbiblical teaching has caused some to believe that saved people die and become God's angelic hosts, giving them the same unlimited travel potential as God's appointed messengers.

The Bible is clear concerning the deaths of the righteous. All spirits of men, women, and children are transported out of their physical bodies and assigned to "rest" until the resurrection of the dead in Christ at the time of the gathering together of the church. At this present time, any believer who died in covenant with Christ is gathered with the saints of all ages in a special paradise. The word "paradise" is used three times in the New Testament: when Christ told the dying thief on the cross, "Today you will be with me in paradise" (Luke 23:43); when Paul wrote that he was in the third heaven and saw paradise (2 Cor. 12:1–4); and when Christ promised the church of Ephesus that if they overcame and entered heaven victorious, they would "eat of the tree of life, which is in the midst of the paradise of God" (Rev. 2:7).

In paradise, the human spirit maintains all five senses that existed in the physical realm and has the same physical appearance that it had while abiding in the body. Since the resurrection of the dead has not yet occurred, there have been departed believers entering the heavenly dwelling for over 1,900 years. They have never aged in their spirit bodies but are not angelic in nature. They will be clothed in their new body at the moment of the resurrection of the dead in Christ.

In the Biblical account of the return of Christ, references allude to the saints, or individual believers who have overcome and are victorious. Paul wrote that Christ would return with "all of his saints" (1 Thess. 3:13), and that when He comes, He would be "glorified in his saints" (2 Thess. 1:10). At Christ's return to earth, the "armies in heaven followed him on white horses, clothed in fine linen clean and white" (Rev. 19:14). However, there are other verses dealing with the return of Christ that mention Him coming with "his mighty angels...taking vengeance on those who do not know God" (2 Thess. 1:7–8). Christ at His return to set up His kingdom will send His angels with the sound of a trumpet to gather His elect (Matt. 24:31).

Angels are God's eternal beings from the beginning of creation, and the saints are the resurrected believers whose spirits were given a new glorified body at the resurrection of the dead. Christ will bring the spirits of these individuals from paradise to earth when He returns, as Paul wrote, "For if we believe that Jesus died and rose again, even so them also which sleep in Jesus Christ will God bring with him" (1 Thess. 4:14).

I OFTEN ASKED THE LORD TO PROTECT MY FAMILY BUT A CHILD WAS KILLED. DID GOD LET ME DOWN AND WHY?

Many godly men and women have experienced the death of a child. Oral Roberts lost his oldest son in a tragedy. Oral's daughter and son-in-law were killed in a plane crash, and his son Richard lost a child shortly after it was born. Yet Oral had tremendous results in praying for and seeing miracles. Elisha received a "double portion" of Elijah's anointing, and at death, his bones raised a dead soldier. Yet, the Bible says, he died of a sickness. If his bones raised the dead, why couldn't the anointing heal him?

It is possible for a good person to be in the wrong place at the wrong time, or for a prayer burden to be ignored. In the busyness of life, we can miss the voice of God helping us prevent future trouble. Often, good people ignore "warning signals" or those deep-felt burdens, and override them to their own demise. Any strong burden in your spirit is a sign of some danger or problem on the horizon. If we ignore senses of danger and go ahead with our plans, we cannot blame God if something goes wrong.

When Paul boarded a ship headed to Rome, he warned the captain they shouldn't go because there were winter storms on the Mediterranean and the journey would be dangerous. The captain ignored Paul, and in the middle of their trip a massive typhoon hit, and without angelic intervention, Paul and the entire ship with over 200 on board would have sunk in the sea!

In the early church, James died and Peter was spared. God did not love Peter more than James. However, the church heard of the death threat, prayed nonstop, and experienced a spiritual breakthrough on Peter's behalf.

Paul escaped danger on numerous occasions, described in Acts, including being lowered in a basket over a wall in Damascus, escaping at night on horseback from a death threat, and surviving a shipwreck and a poisonous snakebite, yet he was beheaded in Rome and not rescued from the jail as Peter was. At first, Paul said he knew God was able to deliver him, and in his final epistle written to Timothy, he said he was "now ready to be offered," meaning he was accepting his martyrdom.

In Hebrews 11, Paul lists the faith heroes of the Bible. He speaks of the miraculous feats and answers to prayer they experienced. He then speaks of others who were not rescued and were tortured and died. He said they did not accept deliverance but desired a "better resurrection," which alludes to a martyr's crown, the highest level of sacrifice.

There could be various reasons why bad things happen, and there is not one simple explanation. However, when a friend of mine lost a beautiful daughter in a plane crash, a fellow minister who experienced that same tragedy called him. He was told not to begin questioning why, as he would ask that the rest of his life. He was told that only the Lord knew things about the accident that no one else understood and those questions would be answered one day in eternity.

CHAPTER EIGHT

ANGELS OF BLESSINGS

When we speak of blessings, we often think only of people being blessed. However, in the Scripture, many different things can come under the influence of God's blessings. A woman who is barren can become fruitful with children (Gen. 17:6; Ps. 113:9). Children are blessed by the Lord through His Spirit (Isa. 44:3). The homes of those who support ministry are blessed (Ezek. 44:30). God promised to bless the animals on a farm of those who follow Him (Deut. 7:13). Those who practice the giving of tithes and offerings are targeted for God's blessings (Mal. 3:10). The works of our hands are blessed (Deut. 15:10). The Psalmist wrote that the Lord would bless His people out of Zion (Ps. 128:5) and bless those who would bless Israel (Gen.12:3).

Angels are not just messengers to announce prophetic events, or bring warnings, judgment, or encouragement to a person. From specific verses in Scripture, angels are also in a position to release specific blessings upon those who follow the Lord.

The Blessing of Abraham

One of the best examples of the blessings through angels can be found in the life of Abraham and his descendants. God's plan was to separate Abram from his relatives in Ur (the area of modern Iraq), bring him into Canaan land (later called Israel), and through his future son Isaac, birth a new nation that would serve the true God and, eventually, maintain a godly lineage for the future Messiah, Jesus Christ.

Jewish tradition teaches that Abram's father, Terah, was an idol worshipper, yet Abram convinced him to depart from the city of Ur and join him in this new journey. The family traveled to Haran (located in Turkey). After Terah's death in Haran, Abram left the region and journeyed to Canaan land. The Lord began appearing to Abram, and each time, Abram built altars, offering sacrificial offerings to God (Gen. 12:7). Years later, after a brief war, "the Lord appeared to Abram in a vision" (Gen. 15:1), cutting a covenant with Abram which sealed God's promises to Abram that his descendants would inherit the land.

The first Biblically recorded angelic appearance was to Hagar, the personal handmaiden of Sarah, Abraham's wife. The angel visited Hagar predicting she would birth a son named Ishmael whose descendants would in the future expand into a multitude. He would also be a "wild man" with a disposition to war against others (Gen. 16). After Ishmael's birth, "the Lord appeared to Abram and commanded him to walk perfect before Him as He planned to make Abram a great nation." This was when God changed his name from Abram (meaning "exalted father") to Abraham, which identified him as a father of a multitude. In Genesis 18, the Lord and "two men" (actually two angels), met with Abraham to confirm that within one year Sarah would conceive a son called Isaac.

When Isaac was a boy, God tested Abraham, saying to him, "Take now thy son, thine only son Isaac, whom thou lovest, and get thee into the land of Moriah; and offer him there for a burnt offering upon one of the mountains which I will tell thee of" (Gen. 22:2). Abraham obeyed, going where God commanded, he built an altar to sacrifice his son. But an angelic messenger appeared when Abraham prepared to lay Isaac on the altar.

And the angel of the Lord called unto him out of heaven, and said, Abraham, Abraham: and he said, Here am I. And he said, Lay not thine hand upon the lad, neither do thou any thing unto him: for now I know that thou fearest God, seeing thou hast not withheld thy son, thine only son from me. (Gen 22:11–12)

Then God provided a ram for Isaac's substitute.

When Isaac was in his late thirties and not married, Abraham was concerned about the right woman for him. He depended upon the same angel who had led him into the Promised Land to go before his servant and choose the perfect match. He told his servant, "He [God] shall send His angel before you…" (Gen. 24:7). The servant was concerned the woman would not follow him back to Canaan to marry Isaac (Gen. 24:39). Abraham again reiterated, "The LORD, before whom I walk, will send His angel with you and prosper your way; and you shall take a wife for my son from my family and from my father's house" (Gen. 24:40–44 NKJV).

When the servant arrived at the exact location and met Rebekah, he explained to her father her assignment, and also made it clear that God had sent His angel to prosper him in what he did (Gen. 24:40). The servant asked for a strange sign that would confirm to him that the Lord had selected the right virgin girl. Abraham's servant had ten camels that needed food and water, and if the woman at the well would care for the camels, she would be the perfect girl for Isaac. All that was in his heart she performed (Gen. 24:42–46). This was truly a "marriage made in heaven," as Isaac was the son of promise, and his future wife would be responsible for two sons, one named Jacob, who would then have twelve sons and initiate the birth of Israel.

Following the Trail of a Blessing

When reading the stories of Jacob, there was a specific angel that was with him, even in the times when he was a trickster and deceiver. In Genesis 25, Jacob snatched his brother Esau's birthright and tricked his father, Isaac, to receive Esau's firstborn blessing (Gen. 27). Esau, in anger, intended to kill Jacob. However, Jacob's mother, Rebekah, sensed the threat, and sent Jacob far from home into exile, to her brother Laban's home in Syria. There, Jacob lived twenty years, married Laban's daughters, Leah and Rachel, and was blessed with eleven sons (Benjamin was born later near Bethlehem). Angels were active from the beginning to the conclusion of Jacob's exile.

In a dramatic dream, shortly after fleeing from home to head into displacement, Jacob dreamed of a ladder reaching the top of heaven with angels ascending and descending to earth. God promised to return Jacob to the Promised Land, and in return, Jacob promised God a tenth (tithe) of his resources when the Lord fulfilled this promise (Gen. 28:12–22).

When the Lord released Jacob, an angel appeared and explained how God observed Laban's mistreatment of him. God blessed Jacob's labor because of the vow he made following the ladder dream twenty years ago. God's word was "leave Syria with your flocks and family and return to your home land" (Gen. 31:1–18). Laban was angry when he learned that Jacob slipped the family out secretly, leaving him unable to say good-bye to his daughters and his grandchildren. Laban pursued Jacob with the intention of harming him, until God appeared to warn him not to speak any evil concerning Jacob (Gen. 31:24). This was not the conclusion of angelic involvement in Jacob's life.

After leaving Laban and entering the covenant land
of God, we read, "And Jacob went his way and the angels
of God met him" (Gen. 32:1). Jacob saw and called them
"God's hosts," meaning God's army. This angelic group
was to provide assistance to Jacob, knowing that Esau
would show up with four hundred men (Gen. 32:1–6).
Once Jacob entered the land that was promised to Abraham and Isaac, he was fearful of meeting Esau, knowing
his brother could kill him and his entire family.

As part of his restoration with Esau, Jacob prepared
a large "gift" to present to his estranged brother: a portion of the animals that Jacob had herded from Laban's
farm. He had not stolen these animals—they were a part
of his wages paid to him for working for twenty years.
After preparing this offering and before meeting Esau,
Jacob suddenly encountered an angel whose words and
actions would forever change his life and destiny:

> And Jacob was left alone; and there wrestled a
> man with him until the breaking of the day. And
> when he saw that he prevailed not against him, he
> touched the hollow of his thigh; and the hollow of
> Jacob's thigh was out of joint, as he wrestled with
> him. And he said, Let me go, for the day breaketh.
> And he said, I will not let thee go, except thou
> bless me. And he said unto him, What is thy name?
> And he said, Jacob. And he said, Thy name shall

be called no more Jacob, but Israel: for as a prince hast thou power with God and with men, and hast prevailed. (Genesis 32:24–28)

This wonderful encounter occurred one night before Jacob came face-to-face with Esau. This angel of the Lord changed Jacob's name to Israel and touched his thigh, giving him a limp for the rest of his life. Jacob was always on the run and his "limp hip" would slow him down so he could no longer run from men or God!

Note the number of times and places where an angel or a host of angels were a part of his dreams and life:

- Jacob dreamed the dream of the ladder of blessing with the angels of God (Gen. 28:12).
- An angel visited him in Syria telling him to return to the Promised Land (Gen. 31:11–13).
- The angels met him prior to meeting Esau (Gen. 32:1–2).
- Jacob wrestled an angel of the Lord and received a spiritual transformation (Gen. 32:24–25).

The blessing of Jacob was undeniable. He left home with nothing and found a job with his mother's brother in Syria. He worked diligently and eventually left with twelve children and countless animals. In twenty years, God had changed the heart of his brother, Esau, and when they met, Jacob told Esau to take the gift of animals, because he "had enough" (Gen. 33:10–11). Even his father-in-law, Laban, understood the power of the blessing when he said, " 'Please stay if I have found favor in your eyes, for I have learned by experience that the LORD has blessed me for your sake.' Then [Laban] said, 'Name me your wages, and I will give it' " (Gen. 30:27–28 NKJV).

Jacob then confessed to Laban, "For what you had before I came was little, and it has increased to a great amount; the LORD has blessed you since my coming" (Gen. 30:30 NKJV).

Jacob was an older man and his sons were grown and having their own children when he finally met Joseph in Egypt. While there, Joseph married and his wife birthed two sons: Manasseh, meaning "God has made me to forget my struggle and toil" (Gen. 41:51), and Ephraim, meaning "the Lord has made me fruitful in the land of my affliction" (Gen. 41:52). Joseph's sons would be adopted into the family, and both of their descendants would be given a land grant, once Israel repossessed the Promised Land under Joshua. Jacob would long be entombed with his people when Israel would depart back home. Yet Jacob prayed and asked the angel to go with his grandsons and make them a multitude in the earth (Gen. 48:16).

In Psalms 103:20, it is written: "Bless the Lord, you his angels, who excel in strength, who do his word, heeding to the voice of his word."

Meeting an Angel of Blessing

Angels continue to bring blessings to us today, as illustrated by a most amazing event that occurred to my VOE office manager's sister. I have asked her to relay this for you:

> In April of 1999, I was engaged to be married to Jeremy Reid. We had saved money for over a year and found the perfect starter home for Jeremy to live in until our wedding in August. Because the house was in a rural area where there was a volunteer fire department, the department required proof that the local fire dues were paid before we could close on the house. The day before we were to close and pay the fire dues, our broker called and informed us that we needed an additional $400 for closing the next day.
>
> I knew we did not have the money and our parents could not assist because they were paying for the wedding. I stopped and prayed and told the Lord that I knew this was supposed to be our house, and that somehow I would pay those fire dues and He would just have to work it out for me. After arriving at the fire station, they told me that I needed to get a number from a plaque that was posted on a tree in the yard, which they used to identify who paid their dues. I drove to the house and was standing in the front yard looking at the

plaque when suddenly a man pulled into the driveway. I was frightened because I was alone and he was a very large man. He exited his car and came straight towards me in one swift movement and said, "The Lord told me to give this to you." He pulled a large amount of cash from his pocket and handed it to me. Before I could respond, he was back in his car and out of the driveway! I immediately headed to my car to follow him. As he went around the curve, it was as though he simply disappeared! I drove around looking for him and found neither him nor the car.

When I finally stopped, I counted the money and was stunned to discover twenty $20 bills. I had not told anyone about needing the additional money, so I joyfully headed to my parents' house to tell my mom about this strange answer to prayer. After going in, I passed a picture of my grandparents on the mantel, which I had passed many times over the years. This time I stopped cold when I looked at the picture and saw who appeared to be the same man who had handed me the money. He looked exactly like my grandfather, who had died before I was born. I never knew him or my grandmother, but the look was identical.

To this day I cannot understand how God did this or who the person was, but to me, it was a messenger of the Lord—perhaps an angel that took on a human appearance and brought me the miracle I needed to meet my needs at that moment!

ARE ANGELS GENERATIONAL, IN THE SENSE THAT THEY REMAIN WITH ONE FAMILY FOR GENERATIONS?

I will answer this from two opposing sides. In the spirit world, there is a type of spirit known as a "familiar spirit," mentioned sixteen times in the Old Testament. They operate through witches and sorcerers as indicated in 1 Samuel 28, when the witch of Endor attempted to contact the dead through a familiar spirit. They can be familiar with people, places, and situations and connected with an unconverted family for generations. This could be a clue as to why certain sins continue in a family for generations, as these spirits create strongholds of bondage.

Concerning angels, when Jacob was blessing Ephraim and Manasseh, he prayed: "The Angel which redeemed me from all evil, bless the lads; and let my name be named on them, and the name of my fathers Abraham and Isaac; and let them grow into a multitude in the midst of the earth" (Gen. 48:16).

Jacob requested that the angel who was with him continue to bless and be with the next generation. There was a special angel with Abraham, too, and we see steady angelic activity in the life of Jacob. There is no reason to believe that these were two different angels, but instead an angel assigned to the early patriarchs who gave instruction, warnings, and direction to ensure that the will of God would be completed.

God thinks generationally. When He gave Abraham the promise of a future nation, He said the blessing would be passed to Abraham's "seed," which refers to his descendants (Gen.12:7, 13:15, 15:18). He promises blessings to you, your children, and their children's children (Ezek. 37:25; Acts 2:39). It is possible a generational angel can be assigned to a godly family.

CHAPTER NINE

ANGELS OF SPIRITUAL WARFARE

A good question has been asked: If there are over 7 billion people on earth, how could everyone have an angel? The answer is "everyone" does not have an angel. If they are in a false religion, worship idols, are not in covenant with God, or are wicked or evil, there is no godly protection assigned over them.

The Shepherd of Hermas is an ancient text from the second century AD. This vision was considered by many of the early church theologians as inspired, and was commonly read in the early church to believers. Without going into too much detail about the vision, the seer, a shepherd, mentions a guardian angel that protects each believer against an opposing agent of the devil, who is assigned to hinder each person. Concerning this thought, the shepherd speaks with an angel. The manuscript reads:

There are two angels with a man—one of righteousness, and the other of iniquity. And I said to him,

"How sir am I to know the powers of these, for both angels dwell with me?" "Hear," he said, "and understand them. The angel of righteousness is gentle and modest, meek and peaceful. When therefore he ascends to your heart, forthwith he talks to you of righteousness, purity, chastity, contentment and every righteous need and glorious virtue. When all of these ascend into your heart, know that the angel of righteousness is with you. These are the deeds of the angel of righteousness…"*

Angels are not with a person twenty-four hours a day and can move at the speed of thought, and one angel could perform perhaps thousands of assignments in a single day. Angels do not just stand and watch you study, eat dinner, or take a shower in the morning. They minister to specific needs and situations or protect from danger and premature death.

An example is found in Daniel. Angels were present only when he needed to understand a vision, and when he faced death in Babylon in the lions' den, and when his three companions were thrown in the furnace of fire. A "fourth man" was observed in the flames, who was an angel protecting the man from being burned to death (Dan. 3:25).

---

* *The Shepherd of Hermas*, in *Ante-Nicene Fathers*, vol. 2, p. 266.

Countless Angels

Saint Athanasius (c. 296–373) was an influential leader who was also known as the "Father of Orthodoxy," or as some Protestants label him, the "Father of the Canon." He wrote, "For there are many Archangels, many thrones, and Authorities, and dominions, thousands of thousands and myriads of myriads, standing before him, ministering and ready to be sent."*

Saint Athanasius based the number of angels on a verse in Revelation 5:11: "Then I looked, and I heard the voice of many angels around the throne, the living creatures, and the elders; and the number of them was ten thousand times ten thousand, and thousands of thousands" (NKJV).

Based on the information available in Revelation 5, around God's throne there are twenty-four elders (Rev. 5:8) and four living creatures (Rev. 5:14). Many believe the redeemed saints are in heaven singing the chorus John heard, "Worthy is the lamb..." (Rev. 5:12). If these voices, however, are the host of heaven, angels, there are "ten thousand times ten thousand and thousands of thousands." If taken literally, the number here is 100 million. John then adds "and thousands of thousands." In reality, he is stating that the number of the heavenly hosts cannot be measured.

---

* "Discourse II Against the Arians," in *Nicene and Post-Nicene Fathers*, chap. XVII, ser. II, vol. 1, p. 362.

Daniel saw a similar vision of heaven and the angels, and said, "Thousand thousands ministered unto him, and ten thousand times ten thousand stood before him" (Dan. 7:10). Psalms 68:17 expands on this thought by saying, "The chariots of God are twenty thousand, even thousands of angels…" The prophet Micaiah saw a vision with God sitting on his throne, and the host of heaven on his left and right side (2 Chron. 18:18). In the book of Job, the writer describes a heavenly counsel meeting with the "sons of God" (angels) and Satan, the accuser, was mingling among them (Job 1:6–7). The point is clear: There is no shortage of angels to battle demonic assignments and minister to the saints.

Angels become involved in battling the Satanic forces of darkness. In Daniel 10, there were two principal spirits that attempted to exercise dominion over the government leaders of Persia, called the "prince of the kingdom of Persia" (Dan. 10:13), and also a second spirit that would be involved with the future empire of Greece, called "the prince of Grecia" (Dan. 10:20). The angel told Daniel he "remained with the kings of Persia" (Dan. 10:13). The angel further revealed that when he concluded speaking with Daniel, he would return to fight with the prince of Persia, who was the demonic entity ruling over Persia. When the battle concluded and the angel departed back to heaven, then the prince of Greece would come. This historically occurred many years later, when Alexander the Great, the Grecian military general and king, overthrew the kings of Persia, setting up his headquarters in Babylon.

Spirits in the Home

The early civilizations were knowledgeable of the existence of a spirit world. In ancient Mesopotamia, people would place symbols and, at times, gods at the entrances of their homes and temples, to prevent the wrong spirits from entering their house. During the Exodus, the lamb's blood was applied to the left, right, and top posts of the outer doors to prevent the angel of death from entering the home and taking the life of the firstborn (Exod. 12). Once the twelve tribes entered the Promised Land, they were to mark the post of their homes with the Word of God (Deut. 6:9). This law eventually led to the creation of a mezuzah, a small object that contains rolled parchments of Scripture that is attached to the right side of the front door of a devout Jewish home.

Evil spirits possess people and their homes. According to Christ, when an unclean spirit departs from a person, either willfully (by its own choice) or by being "cast out" (Mark 6:13), the evil spirit seeks to return with seven other spirits more wicked than himself, entering in and dwelling in the "house" he initially departed from (see Matt. 12:43–45). The Greek word used for "house" in the passage in Matthew is *oikos*, and can literally or figuratively mean "a family." When the adversary controls one family member, they can impact the entire family, or the "house." Spirits are not interested in dwelling in an empty old building, as the television series of *Ghost Hunters* implies. Spirits desire a human body.

When the Hebrew nation of 600,000 men and their families departed from Egypt, God Himself had initiated plagues that were in reality a direct attack upon Egypt's false gods, to prove to the Egyptians that not only was the Hebrew God superior to Egypt's dead deities, but Yahweh was the only true God in existence. The Hebrew tribes were to repossess the land of their fathers Abraham, Isaac, and Jacob, and were forbidden to mingle their religious beliefs with surrounding pagan tribal idols. God forbade the people from any form of idolatry, especially bringing idols into their homes. One reason He did so was because idols attract evil spirits and open an entrance to the home of those who bring recognition or worship to such false objects.

Many believers unknowingly crack open an entryway for demonic activity in their homes by the very things they allow inside. Those who have formally been involved in Satanic or occult activity or in false religions are more aware of this than those raised in church.

When Joshua and Israel conquered Jericho, there was a warning given to the soldiers not to personally take any objects from the city for themselves: "And you, by all means abstain from the accursed things, lest you become accursed when you take of the accursed things,

and make the camp of Israel a curse, and trouble it"
(Josh. 6:18–19 NKJV). Jericho was the first of approxi-
mately thirty-one Canaanite cities that Joshua and the
Hebrew warriors conquered. All the spoils gathered during this conquest were to be given to the treasury of the
Lord's Tabernacle as a first fruits offering: "But all the
silver and gold, and vessels of bronze and iron, are conse-
crated to the LORD; they shall come into the treasury of
the LORD" (Josh. 6:19 NKJV). The first fruits belong to the
Lord, and if withheld, not only are they cursed, but all of
Israel would be "accursed" (Josh. 6:18–19). If Jericho's
first fruits were withheld, then the object(s) become a
curse and not a blessing. One man in ancient Israel was
soon to discover that bringing accursed things into your
dwelling place can cost you not only the "victory," but
eventually your life!

During the conquest of Jericho, a man from the tribe
of Judah, Achan, secretly seized some gold bars and a
beautiful Babylonian garment and hid them in his tent.
As a result, when the Hebrew troops engaged in their
second military campaign at a small city named Ai, several Israelites were slain and Israel experienced defeat.
In frustration, Joshua reminded God that He had not
kept His word that Israel would defeat all her enemies
(Deut. 11:25). God commanded Joshua to "get up" and
listen, and revealed the reason for Israel's defeat. Someone had disobeyed God's instruction and was hiding
accursed things among his possessions. Only when the

sin of Achan was exposed, the cursed items removed from Achan's tent, and Achan was held accountable and stoned to death by the people of Israel, was God's blessing restored and Israel defeated her enemies (Josh. 7:24–26, 8:1–2).

Angelic Reinforcements

Believers know that our spiritual authority over all the powers of the enemy is found in three warfare resources. First is the power of the Word of God. During his temptation, Jesus quoted three Scriptures located in the Torah (from Deuteronomy), to counter Satan's temptation. The Word became a "sword" of the Spirit (Heb. 4:12). The second weapon is the power of the blood of Christ. Christ's blood is the source of redemption and all spiritual blessings. Satan is overcome by the blood of Christ (Rev. 12:11). The third weapon for spiritual warfare is the second half of Revelation 12:11: We "overcome . . . by the word of our testimony." The word for "testimony" here, in Greek, is *maturia*, and refers to judicial evidence. It is testimony given by a witness in court. These three spiritual resources—the Word, the blood of Christ, and the word of our testimony—are significant as angels are attracted to these spiritual weapons. Just as unclean spirits are attracted to those things related to sin, the flesh, and the spiritually and morally unclean, the presence of the Holy Spirit and the angels of the Lord are attracted to the Word of God, to the worship of God, and to prayer.

Since angels respond to the voice of the Lord and to God's Word, it is important that when confessing and "claiming" a promise that we speak God's Word out of our mouths and place it deep within our hearts. After Christ was tempted three times and he quoted three passages from Deuteronomy in response to Satan's temptations, angels came and ministered to him (Matt. 4:11). Throughout history, angels have battled Satanic forces, and in every instance, the angel came out on top, and they will continue to do so!

WHY DO PEOPLE SEEM TO ENCOUNTER DEMONIC SPIRITS MORE THAN ANGELS?

This question is interesting and does appear to be true. Before they became believers, many Christians describe seeing some form of dark spirits, either as dark shadows in the form of a man, or a manifestation of an evil spirit, yet few believers have actually seen an angel of the Lord.

The first reason that comes to mind is that angels carry not only the presence of God, but the *holiness* of God. There are living creatures and seraphim angels continually standing before God's throne crying, "Holy, holy, holy, is the Lord" (Rev. Isa 6:1–4). Holiness denotes being separated and set apart, meaning God is superior, and set apart from all other "gods." Old Testament holiness required a cutting apart from what was unclean, either in character or in ritual form. Certain foods and actions were unclean. God's holiness denotes His moral and spiritual perfection and His willingness to judge righteously mankind's imperfections.

When angels appeared to Moses in the burning bush in the Median desert and to Joshua near Gilgal in Jericho, they demanded that these men remove their shoes, as the ground they were on was "holy." There was nothing "holy" about the actual ground, other than the angels being present on it. Thus the angel made the ground holy.

Demons, on the other hand, are unclean, and attracted to sin or our sin nature. Because the works, character, and nature of mankind lean toward disobedience and sin, there are more open doors and portals for demon spirits to enter. Although these spirits are invisible, the veil on the eyes of individuals must be lifted to see into the spirit world. Certain drugs seem to open a portal in the brain that enables people to see the invisible world. At times, the Lord allows us to see demonic powers to acknowledge the actual spirit behind the struggle. Both totally unconverted individuals and backsliders have seen demon entities, and when they did, great fear overcame them. They turned to God and understood the reality of the spirit world and what they were battling.

Angels are more apt to manifest when a person is dedicating themselves to God's service through fasting and prayer, or when the presence of the Holy Spirit is strong and individuals are in a condition of humility and repentance, which is the doorway to holiness or the separation of the base elements of this world.

CHAPTER TEN

ANGELS WHO ENACT JUDGMENT

The book of Daniel is considered an apocalyptic book of the Bible. The terms "apocalyptic" and "apocalypse" refer to sacred Biblical literature that uses unusual symbolism to conceal the true meaning of the text. Within the prophetic books of Daniel and Revelation, angels play a significant role in bringing understanding to the symbolism or knowledge of specific dreams or visions given to the prophetic seer.

In the book of Daniel, God sends delivering angels to close the mouths of lions, preserving Daniel from being a late-night meal for the hungry "king of the beasts" (Dan. 6:22). In a second amazing deliverance, a protective angel prevents three Hebrew men from becoming a pile of ashes in a furnace of fire (Dan. 3:28). Angels are also commissioned to bring specific messages to the prophets, including, in Daniel's case, insight into the far future and on the future Antichrist, his ten kings, and the final kingdom formed on earth before Christ returns.

Angels as Watchers

The early and later parts of the book of Daniel were written in Hebrew. However, a large portion was written in Aramaic, as it was a common language spoken throughout the Assyrian and Babylonian Empires. Three times in Daniel, the Aramaic word for "watcher" is used for a guardian angel, in 4:13, 17, and 23. The word in Aramaic is *iyr,* and the other phrase used is "holy one," which in Aramaic is *qaddiysh.* The word alludes to one who "watches, or is awake."

The first reference to angels assigned to keep a continual "watch" is found immediately after Adam and Eve were expelled from the Garden of Eden. God placed cherubim with a flaming sword to guard the entrance to prevent Adam, Eve, or their future descendants from reentering the garden and eating from the tree of life, thus living forever in a sinful condition (Gen. 3:22–24). These special angels turned in every direction—north, south, west, and east—to prevent any living person from gaining access to the tree of life.

The watcher story in Daniel begins with King Nebuchadnezzar. This famous king of Babylon had constructed the most elaborate city in world history, up to his time. He had led his armies into Judea for personal purposes, to capture the smartest Jewish youth, who were then placed under supervision in the king's court. They were to be taught the Aramaic languages, providing the

king with the ability to communicate to the Jewish people, most of whom spoke Hebrew. Nebuchadnezzar had
also seized a long list of gold, silver, and bronze treasures,
and placed them in his Babylonian treasure houses. (For
a list, see Jeremiah 51–52.) The arrogant king burned
the temple of Solomon to the ground and left God's holy
city in smoking ruins. He followed up by chaining up the
Jewish captives and leading them on about a four-month
walking journey, 900 miles away into Babylon.

Long ago in Israel's early history, God spoke to Abraham's descendants and revealed that He would bless
those that blessed Israel, and He would curse those
that cursed Israel (Gen. 27:29). Years after Jerusalem's
destruction, Nebuchadnezzar was troubled by a night-
mare in which he saw a large tree covered in fruit with
birds resting on its branches. He heard a voice telling a
"watcher" to cut down the tree but leave the stump in
the ground: "I saw in the visions of my head upon my
bed, and, behold, a watcher and a holy one came down
from heaven; He cried aloud, and said thus, Hew down
the tree, and cut off his branches, shake off his leaves,
and scatter his fruit: let the beasts get away from under
it, and the fowls from his branches: Nevertheless leave
the stump of his roots in the earth…" (Dan. 4:13–15).

In the dream, an angel cut down the tree and then
passed over the stump seven times. Daniel interpreted
the dream as a warning that the king would encounter a
mental breakdown and live like a wild beast in the field

for *seven years*. Eventually, he would recover and return to power. The entire dream was fulfilled one year later (Dan. 4:28–31), when a voice from heaven announced that Nebuchadnezzar's kingdom was taken from him, and he experienced a complete mental breakdown.

The Decree of the Watchers

The most interesting aspect of this amazing historical narrative is the unseen activity occurring in heaven, as angels planned for Nebuchadnezzar's mental breakdown and his removal from power for seven years. The decision was made by a decree in the heavenly courts twelve months before it was enacted.

Daniel informed the king that this dream would occur if he did not repent, as the warning was sealed by "The decree of the Most-High" (Dan. 4:24). God had been observing the actions (pride) of Nebuchadnezzar and his treatment of the holy temple, the holy city (Jerusalem), and the holy people, the Jews: "This matter is by the decree of the watchers, and the demand by the word of the holy ones: to the intent that the living may know that the Most High ruleth in the kingdom of men, and giveth it to whomsoever he will, and setteth up over it the basest of men" (Dan. 4:7).

Two types of angels are referred to in this verse: the "watcher" and the "holy ones." By definition, "watchers" are angels with a specific mission, including personal oversight into select people, nations, or situations. The "holy ones" are basically the holy angels in general. Notice the watcher is to ensure that the decree is enacted, as the king's dream indicated that a watcher would cut down the tree, initiating the loss of mental capability within the king. There was a "demand" placed by the holy ones with the intent of making the king and others know that God Himself is in charge of the affairs of men, as it is written, "He rules in the kingdom of men" (Dan. 4:7).

There is also a possible second interpretation for the phrase "holy ones" that refers to individuals who are set apart for the purposes of God—either a heavenly and an earthly messenger; an angel or a human. In the Torah, the Jewish people are called "a holy nation" (Exod. 19:6). The chamber where God's presence dwells in the tabernacle is the "holy place" (Exod. 3:5). The Sabbath day is called "holy" (Exod. 16:23), and certain garments can be set aside as holy (Exod. 28:2). The sacred anointing oil is also holy (Exod. 30:31). In the rabbinical understanding of the Holiness of God and the ancient temple, something that was less holy could be sanctified and become more holy, but it was sinful for something that was holy to be used in a profane manner.

As for the watchers in Daniel, tens of thousands of Jews were in Babylonian captivity. It may have been the "demand of the holy ones," or the prayers for God's vengeance rising upward from the lips of the Jewish captives themselves, that reached the heavenly court where the prayer decree was presented to God. The judge of the universe sent His verdict in the form of breaking the pride of Babylon's King Nebuchadnezzar.

Death by the Hand of Heaven

When an angel touched Daniel, the physically weak prophet was immediately strengthened (Dan. 10:19). When a ministering angel was released to Christ after his encounter in the wilderness with Satan and in the Garden of Gethsemane during his agony, Christ was supernaturally strengthened in both instances. After wrestling together most of the night, as the sunlight peaked across the rugged mountains, an angel touched Jacob's thigh, giving the patriarch a limp for life (Gen. 32:24–25).

These are examples of what one touch from an angel can do. But what if the angel is sent to bring judgment instead of blessing upon a person? What can one touch from an angel do if they are assigned to bring the kiss of death to the disobedient or the wicked?

One Biblical example is found in Acts 12, when King Herod Agrippa I beheaded James and placed a death sentence upon Peter. James died a martyr. Peter, however, escaped his captors when the church prayed without ceasing and God sent a delivering angel into Peter's prison cell to remove his chains and open all the iron gates leading outside the city. God decreed that it was time to take this murderous Herod Agrippa I from the scene.

Following Peter's supernatural release from prison, Agrippa was invited to a royal celebration on the Mediterranean coast. "And upon a set day Herod, arrayed in royal apparel, sat upon his throne, and made an oration unto them. And the people gave a shout, saying, It is the voice of a god, and not of a man. And immediately the angel of the Lord smote him, because he gave not God the glory: and he was eaten of worms, and gave up the ghost. But the word of God grew and multiplied" (Acts 12:21–24).

The power of one angel to strike death on a massive scale is recorded in the time of King Hezekiah, when the Assyrian army led by Sennacherib made an expedition to attack Jerusalem. The people in the city called a fast and began praying, when suddenly they received a word from God through Isaiah that the Lord would defeat this army without any Israelite fighting against any Assyrian. 2 Chronicles 32:21 reads, "And the Lord sent an angel which cut off the mighty men of valor, and the leaders and captains in the camp of the Assyrians..." Isaiah gives the number of deaths in one night: "Then the angel of the LORD went out, and killed in the camp of the Assyrians one hundred and eighty-five thousand; and when people arose early in the morning, there were the corpses—all dead" (Isa. 37:36–37 NKJV).

Josephus records the details of this historic night of judgment, and identifies the cause for the numerous deaths as a "plague, for God had sent a pestilential distemper upon his army, on the very first night of the siege…" From a rabbinical perspective, this type of judgment is "death by the hand of heaven." This phrase is used when the sin against a person, or in this case against Jerusalem, is so great, that God Himself becomes the judge and officiates a decree directly from His throne and commissions for a swift death to occur and assigns specific angels of judgment to enact it.

This type of death decree can be prevented only through humility and swift repentance, as seen in the Old Testament where the offender presented a sacrifice to God to atone for the wrong. This is illustrated when David sinned by numbering the men of Israel, and did not collect the half-shekel of redemption required by Moses in the law when a census was conducted. This angered God, and He sent a plague to Israel, bringing death to 70,000 men (1 Chron. 21:14). The angel of judgment headed toward Jerusalem with his sword, and God opened David's eyes to see it. The angel instructed David to build an altar on the threshing floor on top of Mount Moriah (known today as the Temple Mount), placing an offering on the sacred altar. The fire of God fell upon the altar, and "The Lord commanded the angel, and he put up his sword again into the sheath thereof" (1 Chron. 21:26–27). The reasoning for the judgment was because when David ignored collecting the half-shekel of redemption from each man, it was as though he said that there is no price for redemption, when in reality God's son, Jesus, would one day pay the ultimate price of his life for mankind's redemption (Gal. 3:13).

Offending Angels

The Scripture indicates it is possible for God the Father to be grieved as He was for forty years during the Israelites' wilderness wanderings. The Holy Spirit can also be grieved as Paul wrote, "Grieve not the Holy Spirit" (Eph. 4). Even Christ felt a sense of grief, manifested when He groaned at the tomb of Lazarus, as the people did not understand His power to raise the dead (John 11:33). If the triune godhead can experience grief when men sin and disobey the Word, can angels also become grieved?

When Israel departed from Egypt and traveled en masse to the Promised Land, a powerful angel was continually with them. God warned Israel not to provoke this heavenly messenger:

> Behold, I send an Angel before thee, to keep thee in the way, and to bring thee into the place which I have prepared. Beware of him, and obey his voice, provoke him not; for he will not pardon your transgressions: for my name is in him. But if thou shalt indeed obey his voice, and do all that I

speak; then I will be an enemy unto thine enemies, and an adversary unto thine adversaries. For mine angel shall go before thee in ... (Exodus 23:20–23)

This angel, called the "Angel of His presence" (Exod. 33:14), was concealed in the cloud during the day and in the fire by night to observe the people continually (Num. 20:16). The sacred name of God was attached to this angel, to the point that if the people provoked him, he would hold their disobedience against them. For this reason, when the ten spies corrupted the entire Israelite camp with unbelief, God sent the entire nation back into the wilderness for forty years, and they were not given a second chance to repent and enter the land. God had warned them the angel of His presence would not forgive them if they offended him. The numerous complaints of the multitude mixed with their unbelief toward God's promises caused a delay in God's purpose for forty years.

For a believer, one of our greatest sins is unbelief; it limits or refuses to believe in the supernatural power and manifestations of God. It is sad to hear individuals who read the same Bible take verses out of context to say that God no longer performs miracles; there are sixty-six books filled with miracles. Do not expect any type of angelic manifestation when a person is filled with unbelief and doubt. The angel of God's presence saw and heard the unbelief of the people, and sent them in circles for forty years.

ARE ANGELS ONLY WITH US DURING DIFFICULT SEASONS?

I believe angels have *access* to us continually, but are not necessarily constantly with us, as the Holy Spirit is the other comforter who will "abide with you forever" (John 14:16) and "dwell with you and shall be in you" (John 14:17). The Holy Spirit has provided prayer language for every Spirit-filled believer, enabling them to pray for the perfect will of God (Rom. 8:26–28), and for Him to intercede when they're burdened or in need. The Holy Spirit assists us in worship, prayer, and understanding the Word of God and life in general. Paul wrote that it is possible to pray in the "tongues of men and of angels" (1 Cor. 13:1), implying that there is a language that angels communicate in that may not be the same as what we use on earth.

The prayer language of the Holy Spirit is our spirit praying to God (1 Cor. 14:4); however, it is possible that the Holy Spirit can and does call on angelic assistance at times. Here's why: God works *in* us and the angels work on the *outside* realm. The Holy Spirit moves upon the heart and the *inner* spirit of a person, whereas angels can work through *outward* circumstances, as they exercise more contact within the natural world, and can be sent from one situation to another. To put it another way, the Holy Spirit's ministry is *inward* and the angelic ministry is *outward*. Angels are not needed every day, but the Holy Spirit is with us every day.

When Peter's chains needed to be broken and the prison door opened, an angel was sent (Acts 12:7). An angel was required to appear to Cornelius, as he was not yet filled with the Holy Spirit to direct him inwardly. Thus, the angel placed him with Peter and the Holy Spirit did the rest of the work as Peter preached the Word. Notice in Acts 10:44–47, the phrase "Holy Ghost" (KJV) is mentioned three times (vv. 44, 45, and 47). The angel is the key messenger in the